Readings in Decentralised Planning

Readings in Decentralised Planning

(With Special Reference to District Planning)

VOLUME II

Edited by

B.N. YUGANDHAR

Director,
Lal Bahadur Shastri
National Academy of Administration,
(Government of India)
Mussoorie

AND

AMITAVA MUKHERJEE

Advisor,
District Planning Unit,
Lal Bahadur Shastri
National Academy of Administration,
(Government of India)
Mussoorie

CONCEPT PUBLISHING COMPANY, NEW DELHI 110059

ISBN 81-7022-348-2 (Vol II)

First Published 1991

Published and Printed by
Ashok Kumar Mittal
Concept Publishing Company
A/15-16, Commercial Block, Mohan Garden
NEW DELHI 110059 (India)

Lasertypeset by
Microtech Advance Printing Systems (Pvt.) Ltd.
H-13, Bali Nagar
NEW DELHI 110015

Readings in Decentralised Planning

(With Special Reference to District Planning)

VOLUME II

Edited by

B.N. YUGANDHAR

Director,
Lal Bahadur Shastri
National Academy of Administration,
(Government of India)
Mussoorie

AND

AMITAVA MUKHERJEE

Advisor,
District Planning Unit,
Lal Bahadur Shastri
National Academy of Administration,
(Government of India)
Mussoorie

CONCEPT PUBLISHING COMPANY, NEW DELHI 110059

ISBN 81-7022-348-2 (Vol II)

First Published 1991

Published and Printed by
Ashok Kumar Mittal
Concept Publishing Company
A/15-16, Commercial Block, Mohan Garden
NEW DELHI 110059 (India)

Lasertypeset by
Microtech Advance Printing Systems (Pvt.) Ltd.
H-13, Bali Nagar
NEW DELHI 110015

In the Honour
of Late Professor
Sukhomoy Chakravarty
A Great
Friend of
our Academy

CONTENTS

LIST OF TABLES

LIST OF PARTICIPANTS/CONTRIBUTORS

1. **Professor B. S. Minhas,**
Distinguished Scientist Emeritus,
Indian Statistical Institute,
New Delhi.

2. **Shri B. N. Yugandhar,** (IAS)
Director,
LBS National Academy of Administration,
Govt. of India, Mussoorie.

3. **Dr. (Mrs.)M. Thaha,**
Director (C. M. P),
National Institute of Rural Development,
Rajendranagar, Hyderabad 500030.

4. **Dr. D. N. Basu,**
Sr. Consultant,
Agro-Climatic Regional Planning Unit,
Sardar Patel Institute of Economic and Social Research,
Ahmedabad.

5. **Mrs. Padma Ramachandaran,**
(IAS) Director,
Institute of Management in Government,
Barton Hill,
Trivendrum 695037.

6. **Professor Milindo Chakravarti**
Department of Economics,
St. Joheph's College,
North Bengal University,
Darjeeling.

7. **Shri R. K. Dar,** (IAS)
Secretary to Govt. of India,
Ministry of Textile,
New Delhi.

8. **Shri V. S. Singh,**
Director, Hill Division,
State Planning Institute,
730, Jawahar Bhawan,
Lucknow (UP)

9. **Mrs. Aneeta Benninger,**
Director,
Institute for Rural Development,
Centre for Development Studies & Activities,
Poona.

10. **Dr. Y. Venugopal Reddy,** (IAS)
Joint Secretary to Govt. of India,
Ministry of Finance,
Department of Economic Affairs,
New Delhi.

11. **Dr. Amitava Mukherjee,**
Advisor, District Planning Unit,
Lal Bahadur Shastri National Academy of Administration,
Mussoorie. (UP)

12. **Dr. S.P. Kashyap,**
Agro-Climatie Regional Planning Unit,
Sardar Patel Institute of Economic and Social Research,
Ahmedabad.

ACKNOWLEDGEMENTS

We are most thankful to the contributors for providing us with their papers. We are particularly grateful to Sardar Tarlok Singh, I.C.S. (Retd.) former Member-Planning Commission, for all the interest, he has taken, and for providing us with the paper on *Panchayati Raj*. Mr. Mohan Kaul, Director, Management Development Programme, Commonwealth Secretariat, London, permitted us to use materials from *Decentralisation for Development* (London: Commonwealth Secretariat) to form parts of Chapter 3 of this book. To him our thanks. Our thanks are due to two anonymous referees for their helpful comments. Our best thanks are due to Dr. Christopher Benninger, Professor & Executive Director, Centre for Development Studies and Activities, Pune for his help, particularly for the cover design for both Volume-I and Volume-II. To Shri R.K. Dar Former-Principal Secretary Hill Department, Government of Uttar Pradesh, and Secretary — Textiles, Government of India New Delhi; Sri Arun Sinha, Joint Secretary to Government of India, Planning Commission, New Delhi and Dr. R.P. Misra, Director Gandhi Peace Research and Professor, Delhi School of Economics Delhi, we a grateful for their support and abiding interest in all our ventures.

We thank the staff of the District Planning Unit, particularly Shri M.K. Tyagi, for his untiring efforts in preparing this volume.

To our friends Ashok, Arvind and Alok we are thankful for their speed of response to our ever pressing demands.

1

WHAT WE DID NOT DEAL

B.N. Yugandhar and Amitava Mukherjee

This is a companion volume for the *Readings in Decentralised Planning* (New Delhi: Concept), 1990, hereinafter referred to as *Readings-I*. After Readings-I went to the press, it was felt that certain aspects of decentralised multi-level planning in India, as discussed in the Readings-I, need reinforcement. We, therefore, decided that a companion volume would make the canvas a complete picture. That provides the justification for preparing the present volume.

Decentralisation, rings very clearly in the Readings-I, but the concept of decentralisation *per se* was not defined, believing it to be so well accepted that it requires no elucidation. The layman, however, who seeks to labour through the volume, may be get lost mid-stream in his attempts to appreciate decentralisation in the context in which it is being discussed without clarity in the concept.

A paper defining decentralisation, decentralised administration, decentralised planning and their inter-connections is, therefore, considered very appropriate for the present volume. This is what the first paper by Mukherjee (Chapter 3 of this volume) seeks to do. Decentralisation on the one hand and decentralised administration and governance, on the other, are inextricably inter-woven.

The papers in Regardings-I were highly optimistic: they showed us the way to a better future in the realm of decentralisation, through a path that may at times be weary, but, they never took us into the "rutt and muck" of the existing scenario, which is important because it is that which provides the base from which to measure variations either way. Thaha's summary of the existing state of affairs in the realm of decentralised planning provides just that base. Instead of a summary of state of arts obtaining in various States, Thaha deals with the otherwise mundane subject "thematically", which makes it readable and emphasises the areas of strengths and weaknesses very appropriately.

Thaha's paper mirrors a mixed picture of success and failures, but elects not to pin-point the major success stories, and not to reason, why that was so. A group of IAS officers examine (in Chapter 6) the three success stories in decentralised planning, namely of Gujarat, Karnataka and West Bengal (stated in alphabetical order) and have tried to figure out the "why and how" of it. This is important for it gives us a fleeting glimpse of how young minds, still not tarnished by the "spoil system", look at the nuances of decentralised planning with which they will probably grapple intensely for the next several years of their lives.

But why is it that despite all our efforts, though much has been achieved, a lot remains to be done. Mukherjee (Chapter 5) attempts at a partial analysis of the causes that inhibit the flourish of political will and administrative inclination to seek a truly decentralised multi-level planning system for our economy. Roy's paper on environment in Readings-I was complete in itself, but the inter-relationship between community of people and community of resources in a system of decentralised planning was not touched upon, by design, because that was beyond the scope of the paper. Nevertheless, the inter-relationship between the community of people and community of resources in a decentralised multi-level planning system has to be emphasised, particularly so in the context of the present day scenario where diminution in the community of resources has reached such a level, that environment has itself been endangered. Mukherjee's paper (Chapter 5) in the current volume seeks to modestly bridge the gap.

The quantum and quality of data are all important, but what is the state of data at the grassroot level state. The current state of affairs of a State, not too well known for decentralised planning, would give the picture without unduly tilting the balance either way. Ramachandran's paper on the state of data in Kerala gives a true and fair account of what prevails now, without being normative.

In the Readings-I the paper by Basu dealt with the entire concept of Agro-climatic Zone. How the exercise on Agro-climatic Zoning could be integrated into the entire gamut of Decentralised Planning has not been discussed. The paper by Basu *et. al.* (Chapter 7) in this volume deals with Agro-climatic Zones and District Planning.

Industrialisation is an issue which is insensitive to planning system. No matter what system of planning is adopted (centralised, pseudo-centralised, or decentralised) industrialisation in some form has to be resorted to. The paper by Dar and Singh brings out beautifully how a district tucked away in the lap of the Himalayas, beautiful but difficult, romantic but fragile, cannot be made to achieve rapid industrialisation without spelling disaster. "It is not possible to create conditions for balanced regional development without a clear and full analysis of and agreement on the pattern of growth which would bring about spatial harmony and equity. "This may be a difficult exercise", they note, but continue that "there is no escape from undertaking it, since the only alternative is totally unregulated growth. In fragile hill regions unregulated growth would sooner or later lead to serious disasters. Methodologies for developing such regional plans", (let us be reminded that district or sub-district plans are also regional plans, depending upon how a region is defined) "are not available off the shelf. For a long time to come", so they believe, "steady progress and improvisation would be necessary to generate methodologies which fit one or another type of hill region". This is a reminder then that quick industrialisation of hill (or for that matter of any ecologically sensitive and environmentally fragile) district must be prepared to have the full blast of developing more poverty and the role of decentralised planning in such conditions ought to clearly earmarked. This is particularly important for people like us who live on the Himalayan range without realising how sensitive it is to our deeds (or misdeeds).

The dynamics of decentralised planning can only be set at the optimal level when, what we call "nuts and bolts" of it are known. This is briefly dealt with by Aneeta Benninger. But then the questions that remain still unanswered *are:* what remains, and what are the issues and problems of the morrow? Venugopal Reddy provides the answer based on his experience as a planner and as an academician.

A discussion on decentralised administration and decentralised planning cannot be complete without a discussion on Panchayati Raj. Sooner than later, the mantle of providing a viable decentralised planning system would rest on the Panchayati Raj Institutions, and notable beginnings have already been made. The paper by IASSI after taking us down the memory lane of Panchayati Raj, tells us the way which Panchayati Raj would take in the days just ahead of us.

But then the "million dollar questions" remain: what are we trying to decentralise ? Why and how well? Minhas's recorded version of his inaugural address to the International Expert Group Meeting on Decentralised Planning at Mussoorie on 11th June, 1990, is a searching criticism to the issues raised by the question and an answer to some of them. We, therefore, begin this volume with the soul-searching wisdom spelled out by Minhas.

It is hoped that the two volumes taken together would cover the wide canvas of decentralised planning quite comprehensively.

succession of years without spelling disaster. It is not possible to even think of, for instance, regional development without a clear and full analysis of, and agreement on the pattern of growth that would bring about spatial harmony and equity. This may be a difficult exercise in many parts but common sense indicates that there is no escape from undertaking it, since the only alternative is totally unregulated growth. In many parts, regions unregulated growth would sooner or later lead to serious disasters. Methodologies for development of such regional plans need to be formulated and targets set. Such plans are not merely regional plans [illegible] depending upon how a region is defined) are not available but [illegible] for a long time to come. Whether however, steady progress and improvisations would be necessary to improve the methodologies which, [illegible] one to need or type of such region. This is a reminder then that most industrialisation, or for that matter of any ecologically sensitive, and environmentally fragile district, must be prepared to have the full hint of developing more powers and a role of a centralised planning in such conditions ought to clearly be examined. This is particularly important for people and those who are on the firm lot as such without realising how people in these places decide for themselves.

The proposals of decentralised planning can only be set at the optimal level when what we call "macro" and "micro" of these are set. This is precisely the key Anjana Jennings. But there are questions that remain still unanswered are: what are the goals and what are the means and problems of these steps? Vitameen Reddi provides the answers based on his experience and planner and as a social scientist.

A discussion on decentralised administration and decentralised planning cannot be complete without a discussion on Panchayati Raj. Some bans and the pattern of providing a viable decentralised planning system would be a great [illegible] Panchayati Raj institutions, and notable beginnings have already been made. The papers by [illegible] after taking up down the memory lane [illegible] [illegible] Raj tells us the way which Panchayati Raj would take in the days that lie ahead.

It is now the difficult and most crucial question: what are we trying to achieve? Why and how will it work? Each volume is a modified version of the inaugural address to the International Expert Group Meeting on Decentralised Planning at Mussoorie on 11th June, 1991, is essentially a concluding address which by the question and an answer to each of them. We, therefore, begin this volume with the essential scheme of questions spelled out by Mathur.

It is hoped that the two volumes taken together would cover the wide canvas of decentralised planning quite comprehensively.

2

DECENTRALISED PLANNING: Centralising What is Already Decentralised?*

B.S. Minhas

Planning is not a substantive discipline and there is no scientific theory of planning. It is at best a tailor's job. Of all the discussion I have heard on decentralisation, it seems that it is really a talk about how to centralise what may really be already decentralised, or what may already be decentralised, is being thought of as centralised, basically because we forget that this area (planning) has no particular theory of its own: it borrows from other disciplines.

Economic activity is organised around the needs and preferences of people, to identify which goods and services are to be produced by enterprises. This is achieved through a system of markets and prices, where markets are organisations and prices are signals. The quantity of goods and services demanded is matched by the quantity of goods and services supplied. There are very strong proofs that the system of markets and prices produces a set of goods which cannot be bettered by any alternative configuration of goods and services produced. That is, a Pareto optimal solution is obtained: in other words, you reach a situation where you cannot increase the welfare of 'A' without hurting the welfare of 'B'. However, markets and prices do not always work: markets often fail and the whole theory of development and planning can really find no niche that if markets fail, can the governments do better; can bureaucratic success really make up for the market failure ? Economists over past 50 years have developed a very satisfactory

* This is the recorded version of the inaugural address delivered at the *International Expert Group Meeting* on *Decentralised Planning* held at the Lal Bahadur Shastri National Academy of Administration, Mussoorie, from 11th to 13th June 1990.

theory of why markets fail, of which one is "externalities", that is, some of the things that we do lead to no reward to us, and some of the things others do, inflict a damage to us about which we can do nothing. There can be externalities on account of asymmetry in information or even on account of incomplete markets. There can be technological externality. Given these, the question is: what shall we do ? When markets fail, we assume that Government intervention may be desirable. But can Governments do better than the market?

While governments have the world over messed up social and economic life, and while there is a theory of market failure, there is as yet no satisfactory theory of government or bureaucratic failure. Worse still, there is no theory of trade off between market failure and government failure; we do not know how to evaluate the trade off between market failure and bureaucratic failure. Only when we have such a theory that we can know how much of market failure to live with and how much government failure to tolerate. Yet whenever markets fail, everyone wants governments to come in, and we know that bureaucrats fail a lot more than markets fail. Even the Soviets have realised this. If one can establish that there is a clear case of market failure, then may be there is a case for bureaucratic intervention, though not always.

We all know that there are economies of scale in power generation; and there may be economies of scale in power distribution. That is, MC < AC all the time, and if you are doing marginal cost pricing, you are making losses all the time. This is a case of natural monopoly and in such cases there is need for government intervention, so that average cost pricing is done or else marginal cost pricing would go on and the output will be far less than what the economy would be wanting. There are instances in monopoly where output is kept at a low level to reap profits. Similarly when, for example, an industry is polluting the environment, though the factory is making money, there is the case of regulating the activity of the factory. Does this mean that government would do better ? The government does not necessarily perform better and because the market has failed, it is not necessary that government would succeed. Hence the criterion to be used is the "double market failure principle." That is, even if one knew that the market has failed, the next question to ask is can some market like arrangement be made or can you make some contract be entered into such that the same some thing can be done, not by the government, but by some agencies outside of government. Control is there, not directly done by the government, but by some kind of a contractual system. Unless the two tests are satisfied there is no argument in economic theory for really going in for government regulation.

Let us now examine the second kind of market failure. Let us take law and order for instance. Everybody thinks that law and order shall be taken care of by the government, but if somehow everyone was allowed some private police, nobody would think that government should take care of law and order. The problem with this arrangement is posed by what is called "stratagic behaviour:" the man who is acting as someone's "police" would jump over to his enemy's side if the latter paid more money, and when someone wants protection he doesn't have it, for there is no enforceable contract. Only when such a situation of market failure takes place and when a contract is not enforceable, that it is necessary to have government intervention; otherwise not.

Now the system of market and prices that is being talked about is an example of horizontal co-ordination that takes place for self interest. In all kinds of command economies, including the planned economies, there are command systems, and all manner of administration also has command systems. In such systems horizontal co-ordination is not possible. So when we talk of decentralised planning and all that, deeper issues needs to be kept in mind: what are the decentralisation of the incentive and disincentive mechanisms we can think of, so that we do not have to think of them after we have failed. Then when we have a state Government, we have a "District Government" and when we put something at the village level we have some sort of "Village Government". In such a situation when you are talking of decentralisation, in fact you are slicing things up in such a fashion that we generate centralised notion at every level, because we do not pay attention to basic issues involved.

If there is a mechanism for people's preference and needs to be made known and made obvious at the district level, then at least the common man's needs are known. But what you find now is that, notwithstanding the above, all the schemes are conceived at the national or State headquarters, which is simply being implemented at local level. Even if only implementation is done at the local level, on the basis of people's voice, things would improve but even this has not happened. In India, the basic urge is that government would do everything whenever the market does not work, though knowing that the government fails. Therefore, we would do well to analyse:

(i) Why we want arrangements;
(ii) Why we want institutions;
(iii) Why we want individual action;
(iv) Why we want collectivity of the kind which do not go against the proper kind of incentive and disincentive practice.

The whole question of rewards and punishment in an automatic sense must inform this kind of exercise, or else present attempts at decentralisation, would be attempts at centralising whatever may look decentralised today. It would be an attempt to share a spoil system through a command mechanism by giving the common people a little voice in terms of powers to look at delinquent school teachers and not-dedicated doctors. Even in States like Karnataka there is no decentralisation because only 10 per cent of the resources are untied and there is no human resource at the local level to implement even those 10 per cent of the resources except perhaps the poorly paid Panchayat Secretary. When you slice the country in this fashion for purely bureaucratic centralisation, of this sort, some old channels of data and information flow gets choked off, damaging decentralisation efforts. Let us not be carried away by such tailoring.

3

DECENTRALISATION : Some Conceptual Issues

Amitava Mukherjee

Introduction

Any discussion of decentralisation, is complicated by terminological problems.[1] The term 'decentralisation' is given a variety of connotation by different users and confusion abounds in respect of the relationship between decentralisation and related terms, including on the one hand 'centralisation' and on the other hand terms such as 'devolution' and 'decentralisation'. Some of these terminological issues need to be clarified which is attempted here.

Decentralisation Defined

Although the term decentralisation is used in a wide range of contexts, we are concerned specifically with decentralisation of planning and decentralisation of government. We wish to define decentralisation here as any change in the organisation of planning and government which involves the transfer of powers or functions from the national level to any sub-national level(s) or from the sub-national level to another, lower sub-national level. This definition is not universally acceptable, because (some prefer a narrower definition, comparable to what we may call here devolution), while other use the terms more broadly to also include the transfer of powers or functions from government organs to parastatal or non-government organisations. It is important to consider decentralisation, whether of government or planning, as a process of change rather than as an end in itself.

Typology of decentralisation

Because the term decentralisation is defined broadly here, it is inevitable that there are many different degrees and forms of decentralisation. When describing or analysing decentralised system of planning and/or government, and especially when trying to compare or classify them, it is useful to ask the following questions:

(a) Which powers or planning functions have been transferred (taking note in particular of the number powers or functions transferred and their nature and significance) ?
(b) How have they been transferred? (e.g. by Constitutional Law or ordinary legislation, or by administrative fiats or merely by informal means)?
(c) To what level have they been transferred (e.g. State, district, Block, panchayats, or village)?
(d) What is the locus of powers at this level (noting in particular whether power is in the hands of:

(i) elected representatives of the people or appointed officials of the government; and
(ii) an individual or a group ?

A variety of terms is used to describe different types of decentralisation, classified according to some or some combination of the foregoing criteria. The distinction between *devolution*, which usually means the legal transfer of powers and/or functions of whatever character they may be, to a locally elected political body, and *deconcentration*, which is the transfer of powers and or functions of whatever character they may be, by administrative means to local representatives of the central government, is very often made. A related term is *delegation*, which signifies transfer of powers or functions to either local government or local representatives of the central government which is undertaken by administrative means that is not irrevocable. The term *dispersal* generally connotes only the posting of personnel outside the national capital, without any significant transfer of powers or functions to them.[2]

Devolution can take place within either a *federal* polity[3] or a *unitary* system[4] of government, and the principal difference between the two is that in a federal system, the powers and functions of the different levels of government are enshrined in the constitution, unlike in a unitary system where they are only embodied in ordinary Acts of the legislature, but there are other differences which are taken into account to distinguish between the two, such as the extent of the power devolved and functions handed drawn, staffing pattern, financial arrangements and the size of the sub-national governments, *states* as in the Indian context. There is a tendency for the states to be relatively large (often as big as individual countries such as Madhya Pradesh and Uttar Pradesh in India) and therefore there is often further decentralisation within each state of a third tier (such as the district) or fourth tier of local government (such as the Blocks in India) or administration and planning, or even beyond (such as the Gram Panchayats). We are concerned here primarily with decentralisation within States in a federal system, since this form of decentralisation is more likely to 'bring decision-makers closer to the people' and thus achieve the main developmental aims of decentralisation.

The definitions given above provide some guidance, but they should be treated with caution because no universally acceptable definition of any of these terms exists and usage can vary considerably. It is more appropriate, therefore, to give a brief description of a particular system being defined, using the questions listed above as framework, instead of attempting at fitting it into a specific category.

It should be noted that, because of the wide variety of criteria that can be applied to classify decentralised systems of planning and government, sweeping generalisations should be avoided about which system is 'more' or 'less' decentralised, for one system may be more decentralised according to one criterion but less decentralised according to another.

Centralisation Versus Decentralisation

Centralisation is frequently regarded as the antonym of decentralisation, in the sense that it is the transfer of powers or functions from sub-national levels of government and planning to the national level, or from a lower to a higher sub-national level, but the inter-relationship between the two is much more complex than is appears because of the many different criteria which can be used to measure decentralisation and therefore centralisation. Thus many changes in the organisational structure involve some elements of centralisation and others of decentralisation and hence any change can not be easily classified as falling into the domain of either 'centralisation' or 'decentralisation'. In these cases, a brief description of the nature of the change is much more useful than a general lable such as 'decentralisation' or 'centralisation'.

No system of planning and administration can be completely centralised or decentralised. Both 'centralisation' and 'decentralisation' can best be "regarded as processes of movement in opposite directions along a continuum which has no clearly definable ends — or, perhaps more accurately, along a series of continuums representing the different criteria which can be used to measure centralisation and decentralisation."

The Role of Decentralisation in Development

Decentralisation has been increasingly advocated by governments, individuals, politicians, international agencies and academics as the grand panacea of development problems, but several decentralisation programmes meet their first battleground in the design or implementation stages because not enough attention is paid to the precise benefits which the particular decentralisation programme is likely to bring about to the community of people and to the problems which may arise in the course of its introduction. A brief review of the role of decentralisation in development, examining the three principal benefits which are anticipated, namely, increase in popular participation, improved management of development programmes and the diminution of secessionist tendencies, and then the problems which may result from decentralisation, are therefore in order.[5]

Decentralisation for Popular Participation

Decentralisation is probably most often advocated as a means of increasing popular participation in decision-making and planning for development, where popular participation may be seen either as a desirable end in itself (a basic human 'right' and an essential component of 'democracy', necessary for the development of the individual's self-esteem) or as a means of improving the formulation of planning, implementation of plans and management of development programmes, by relating them to local needs and increasing local commitment to, and involvement in, the process of planning and implementing development.

A number of problems may be associated with this rationale: *One*, the phrase "popular participation" is in itself a very vague term and it is necessary to establish what sort of participation is intended in a particular situation, and it is particularly important to consider *who* are the people who would participate (rural or urban, rich or poor, minorities or majorities, men or women, young or old) and the *degree* of participation intended (since participation may range from little more than local consultation in planning development projects to managing development effort where the local people has more or less complete command over its own affairs); *two*, it is necessary to consider the nature and extent of decentralisation which is most likely to achieve the desired form of participation, since decentralisation *per se* will not guarantee participation, and *three*, the obstacles to achieving significant participation by the mass of the population are so numerous and forbidding that the decentralisation should not be expected to produce rapid or dramatic results.

Decentralisation and Improvement in the Quality of Development Efforts

As we have seen earlier decentralisation is frequently advocated for improving the management of development programmes by increasing popular participation, but decentralisation can also be seen as a means of improving development management in alternative ways, particularly so it can help to cut delays in decision-making, increase flexibility, increase speed of response to changing conditions, improve coordination between the various agencies or departments involved in development at the level to which powers and functions are decentralised and, cut down administrative and social costs.

But the relationship between decentralisation and improved management is a lot more complex than would appear at first sight. *Firstly*, a decentralisation programme has to be carefully designed and implemented if it is to bring about marked improvements in management of development planning and some decentralisation programmes may actually result in a deterioration in some respects particularly so in their initial stages; confusion over the division of responsibilities and the administration of new procedures are more likely consequences. *Secondly*, improved planning and management (like effective participation) of developmental programmes is not easy to achieve with or without decentralisation because it is function of so many factors, including external events, political expediencies and pressures, and the capabilities and attitudes of individuals, bureaucracy and technical personnel.

Decentralisation as Antidote to Seccessionist Groups

The *third*, important justification for decentralisation is that it reduces pressure from regional groups who are already threatening to secede or may do so in the near future if their demands are not met, in which cases, decentralisation of powers and functions may give these regional groups sufficient command over their own affairs, which would dissude them from seccceding. This rationale often results in federal or 'quasi-federal' forms of decentralisation, within an already decentralised structure. This has been attempted at while dealing with the demands for Gorkhaland in West Bengal and is currently being attempted to contain the Bodoland question in Assam. Whether these will eventually succeed or not will be only borne out by flux of time : it is too early to decide either way, but in these cases we are talking of decentralisation of governance only, which *per se* in not of immediate concern for us.

Decentralisation : Problem Areas

It should be noted that problems are likely to arise if a decentralisation programme is intended to achieve more than one of the above objectives, because there are some conflicts between the different objectives and so the type of decentralisation which is required to achieve one objective may not facilitate the achievement of the other objective(s). In addition the two problems frequently encountered are, *firstly*, difficulties in implementing important national policies when over decentralisation takes place and, *secondly*, increases in inequalities between regions could be aggravated because the more affluent region, such as districts of Western U.P. *vis-a-vis* Eastern U.P., is in a better position to use the decentralised functions and thus improve its position even further. The incidence of all these problems can, however, be reduced (even if not completely eliminated) by careful design and planning of the decentralisation programme. It is apparent thus that the role of decentalisation in development is complex and it is, therefore, necessary to consider very carefully the justification for any decentralisation programme and the problems which may arise from it. Moreover, the impact of a decentralisation programme depends to a very large extent on the way in which it is designed and implemented.

Managing Decentralisation

A fundamental issue underlying any decentralisation programme is how much (if any) of the proposed decentralised system of planning and governance should be embodied in legislation, and whether this legislation should be ordinary legislation or part of the nation's Constitution. On the one hand, the need to clarify the roles and responsibilities to each level of governance and planning thus reducing conflict and confusion, is supportive of the adoption of a detailed legislation, but at once, the need for the system of planning and governance to be flexible and to be capable of modification in the light of experience speak in favour the use of administrative and not legal procedures, or at best, ordinary Act of the Legislature rather than constitutional law. In practice, a lot depends on the political dispensation of the country or the State concerned, including the degree of consensus over the details of the decentralisation programe and the importance attached to law in the political system. In India for instance, planning at district and sub-district levels is not embodied in any law but is carried out under executive authority.

The Geographical Areas to Which Powers are Decentralised

Two fundamental issues relate to the choice of the areas to which powers and functions are to be decentralised, and the determination of the spatial level of decentralisation (including that of decentralising powers and functions to a hierarchy of different levels, rather than all to one level), the number and size of areas, and their boundaries which is often referred to as the problem of "delineation". These are highly volatile issues and the scope for choice is, in practice, limited, but the decisions made in this regard will have a major influence on the effectiveness of the entire decentralisation programme, including the scope for popular participation and the administrative viability of the local levels of governance.[6]

The Division of Powers

The division of powers between the central government and the lower level or regional and/or local tiers of planning and governance, is one of the most important and at once difficult issues in this regard. There are many different kinds of powers: there are powers in relation to different subject areas (education, health, agriculture, public works, etc.); within each subject area, various powers exists relating to policy-making; powers related to implementation (particularly powers to control staff, finance and other resources). When deciding upon the powers to decentralize it is necessary to consider what powers each level needs to have in order to achieve the required objectives. For example, what powers should the central government retain in order to ensure that basic national policies are implemented and that regional inequalities are reduced? And what powers do local institutions need in order to provide relevant and integrated rural development programmes? It is inevitable, however, that views about the division of powers will differ and the decisions which are eventually made are likely to be influenced as much by political forces as by administrative consideration and economic expediency.

Administrative Organisational Structure

The organisational structure at regional and/or local level is closely related to the division of powers and functions, because administrative arrangement is one of the most important resources required by regional and local tiers of governance. There is no point in giving lower tiers the power to take policy decisions without also giving them the power to control the administrative resource required to enforce these decisions into effect. Where powers are devolved to locally elected political bodies, like the Panchayati Raj Institutions in India at the district and sub-district levels, the most fundamental decisions to be taken are whether or not the local governments should employ their own staff and, the extent to which the National Civil Service, like the All India Civil Services, should be decentralised and the way in which this should be done. The machinery for coordinating the various departments of other administrative agencies at the regional or local level, including where appropriate, central and local government administrative staff, is an issue on which a lot of thought needs to go in, which is closely related to the degree of administrative decentralisation, since decentralisation facilitates (although it does not guarantee) 'horizontal' coordination.

Financial Organisation

The issue of control over financial aspects of decentralisation are equally important.[7] History is replete with instances where the impact of the decentralisation programmes has been lost and dissipated because governments at higher levels have not been prepared to decentralize sufficient control over financial resources. This is the fundamental test upon which one can hear the clamber for powers to tax and borrow at the district level in India today.[8]

While deciding the degree and form of financial decentralisation required, it is essential to consider control over both revenue and expenditure. Decisions about *revenue* have important implications both for regional inequalities and for the impact of decentralisation on secessionist movements where decentralisation of governance is sought to reduce secessionism. When considering alternative sources of revenue it is especially important to take cognizance of the relative importance of locally raised revenue and grants (or loans) from the higher levels of government, because reliance on locally raised revenue is likely to favour the richer areas.

Decisions about *expenditure* are more important in determining the form of development which actually takes place, which from the local point of view, means the extent to which local development plans can be flexible and relevant to local needs and priorities, while from the central government's perspective it means the extent to which the central government can retain control over the direction of development at the local level and, therefore, the implementation of its policies. When deciding about control over expenditure, it should be kept in view that there are several different functions related to financial control, including budgeting, controlling the allocation or disbursal of funds, and monitoring the end use of money, namely accounting and auditing. It is usually desirable that all these functions are not performed at the same level.

Decentralisation in Administration /Governance

The relationship between decentralisation of administration/governance and planning can cause some confusion. There is a tendency for the organisation of planning to be considered independently of the political and administrative organisation of government as a whole and, therefore, efforts to decentralize planning within a relatively centralised system of government — or (less often) for centralised planning to be attempted within a highly decentralised system of government is not an uncommon phenomenon. In both the eventualities planning is not likely to influence the course of development because plans are seldom accepted or implemented. This can be attributed to misconceptions about the nature of planning and the relationship between policy-making, planning and implementation. Planning is the process of making decisions about how resources should be used to achieve policy objectives and, therefore, is an integral part of the political and administrative system. It is because of this we have carried out our discussion on decentralisation in governance and in planning concurrently. Thus decentralisation of responsibility for planning a particular activity or project must be accompanied by decentalisation of the power to make and implement decisions regarding that activity or project. Additionally, decentralisation programmes must include provision for a comparable decentralisation of planning capacity, so that the decentralised powers are used as effectively as possible, which should include the development of planning capacity at regional or local level and the introduction of procedures designed to ensure'vertical' coordination between national and regional or local planning.

Implementing Decentralisation Programmes

It is very important that attention is paid not only to the detailed design of a decentralisation programme but also to the way in which it will be implemented. *Firstly*, it is necessary to have political commitment and support for the programme. *Secondly*, it may be necessary to set up a special orgnisational structure at the national level to implement the programme and when the implementation is completed, this organisation (or a modified form of it) may have an ongoing role to play in coordinating relations between national and regional/local government agencies and monitoring the progress and impact of the decentralisation programme. *Thirdly*, the implementation organisation should prepare an implementation plan, whatever the form, specifying the various activities which have to be undertaken, when they have to be undertaken, and by whom. And *finally*, it is imperative to provide orientation and training for all those affected by decentralisation especially personnel at the level(s) to which powers and functions are being decentralised. It should, incidentally, be noted that the four requirements are not unique to decentralisation programmes; they are necessary for the successful implementation of any kind of reform.

NOTES

1. Diana Conyers: *Decentralisation for Development* (London: Commonwealth Secretariate, Marborough House) 1984, which is the basic source.
2. Solomon Kagwe: "Some Major Issues of Decentralised Administration", in *Decentralised Administration in West Africa: Issues and Training Implications* Commonwealth Secretariate: London) 1987.
3. The Indian situation is an example in point.
4. The cases of Zambia, Sudan and Nigeria are examples in point. See *Decentralised Government*, Proposals for Integrated Local Government Administration, (Lusaka : Government Printer) 1979; Mikhtar Alassam: *Decentralisation in Sudan* (Khartoum: Ministry of Culture and Information) 1981; and G.O. Nwankwo :"Management Problems on the Proliferation of Local Government in Nigeria", *Public Administration and Development*, Vol. 4, No. 1, January — March 1984
5. See G.S. Cheema and D.A. Rondinelli (ed): *Decentralisation and Development: Policy Implementation in Developing Countries* (London: Sage Publications) 19883 for a variety of discussion on these issues.
6. See W.B. Stohr and D.R.F. Taylor (ed.): *Development from Above or Below? The Dialectics of Regional Planning in Developing Countries* (Chichester: Wiley) 1981, Particularly the last Chapter.
7. See R.A.W. Rhodes: *Control and Power in Central-Local Government Relations* (Farnborough: Gower) 1981.
8. See *Recommendations*, in B.N. Yugandhar and Amitava Mukherjee (ed.) *Readings in Decentralised Planning*, Vol. I (New Delhi: Concept Publishing Co.) 1991.
9. A.P. Saxena: *Administrative Reforms for Decentralised Development* (Kuala Lumpeer: Asia and Pacific Adminsitration Centre) 1980.

NOTES

1. Diana Conyers, *Decentralisation for Development* (London: Commonwealth Secretariat, Marlborough House) 1984, which is the basic source.
2. Scan Kaweza, "Some Major Issues of Decentralised Administration" in *Decentralised Administration in East Africa, Issues and Training Implications* (London: Commonwealth Secretariat) 1987.
3. The Indian situation is an example in point.
4. The cases of Zambia, Sudan and Nigeria are examples in point. See Republic of Zambia, *Government Proposals for Alternative Local Government Administration*, (Lusaka Government Printer) 1979; Mikhtar Alassam, *Decentralisation in Sudan* (Khartoum: Ministry of Culture and Information) 1981; and O.O. Nwanwo, "Management Problems on the Proliferation of Local Government in Nigeria," *Public Administration and Development*, Vol. 4, No. 1, January — March 1984.
5. See G.S. Cheema and D.A. Rondinelli (ed.) *Decentralisation and Development Policy Implementation in Developing Countries* (London: Sage Publications) 1983 for a variety of discussion on these issues.
6. See W.B. Stohr and D.R.F. Taylor (ed.) *Development from Above or Below? The Dialectics of Regional Planning in Developing Countries* (Chichester: Wiley) 1981 Particularly the last Chapter.
7. See R.A.W. Rhodes *Control and Power in Central-Local Government Relations* (Farnborough: Gower) 1981.
8. See Recommendations in B.N. Yugandhar and Amitava Mukherjee (ed.) *Readings in Decentralised Planning*, Vol. I (New Delhi: Concept Publishing Co.) 1991.
9. A.P. Saxena, *Administrative Reforms for Decentralised Development* (Kuala Lumpur: Asia and Pacific Administration Centre) 1980.

4

STATUS OF MICRO-LEVEL PLANNING IN INDIA*

Dr. M. Thaha

Introduction

In view of the glaring socio-economic disparities and heterogeneity in natural endowments the significance of micro level planning as a mechanism to ensure alround balanced developed have been recognised from the very inception of planning process in the country and consistently advocated from one plan to another. With the introduction of a variety of new programmes for rural development, requiring close coordination with other departmental programmes in the rural areas, the need for decentralisation of planning and development administration to the district and block levels became all the more imperative. Therefore, in the current plan various measures are being adopted by Planning Commission to promote micro level planning in the country.

At the anvil of the Eighth Five-Year Plan it is felt appropriate to look into the progress made by different states in operationalising the micro level planning concepts. It is evident that the priorities assigned by different State governments vary considerably. Consequently, the states are at different stages in micro level planning. The assessment of the current status of micro level planning in different states will indicate the task ahead in operationalising this concept and in turn enable the policy-makers to evolve strategies for promoting it further. With this intention the present study has been taken up with the broad

* This paper was circulated at the *International Expert Group Meeting on Decentralised Planning* held at the LBS National Academy of Administration, Mussoorie, from 11th to 13th June 1990.

objectives of: (1) to review the strategy and approach adopted for micro level planning in different states in terms of functional and financial decentralisation for plan formulation; (2) to examine the machinery available for undertaking plan formulation, implementation and monitoring at the micro level; (3) to assess the task ahead in operationalising micro level planning, and the concomitant policy implications.

Planning Machinery

Availability of institutional infrastructure for shouldering the responsibility of plan formulation and implementation is an important prerequisite for micro level planning. Even though in recognition of the necessity for proper institutional infrastructure a scheme to strengthen it was launched as early as the Fourth Five-Year Plan, still the States are at different stages and have adopted varying patterns. In spite of the prevailing diversity in the arrangements, there are some common features in the structure of planning machinery. This common feature is the existence of two-tier agencies at the district level in most of the states responsible for plan formulation. One agency plays mainly an advisory role whereas the other one which may be called second tier planning machinery is an executive body and hence technical in nature.

The advisory body has different nomenclatures in different states like District Development and Review Board, District Planning and Development Council, etc. The State of Assam is an exception where this body exists only at the Sub-Divisional level which is known as Sub-Divisional Planning and Development Council. These are high power bodies at the district level involving top level officials and elected representatives of the people in the district. In some states like Jammu and Kashmir, Kerala, Rajasthan and Nagaland, the District Collector is the Chairman of this planning body whereas in all other states a Minister of the State cabinet is its Chairman.

In most of the States the District Planning Advisory Body is assisted by an executive committee at the district level which is a compact body. For example, in Bihar this committee is headed by the Divisional Commissioner, in Gujarat by District Collector, whereas in Maharashtra the designated Minister of the State is the head of this committee. Other members of the executive committee are District Development Commissioner, District Planning Officer, the sectoral heads and representative of district lead bank. In Gujarat it has a representative character built into it by the inclusion of the MLA from the district.

The executive committee plays a very pivotal role. The committee scrutinises the financial estimates of different schemes proposed in the plan and also ensures that these are in accordance with the guidelines issued by the government. In Bihar it also fixes the priority, goals and objectives of development at the district level. In Maharashtra it has all powers of the DPDC and can discharge all functions of DPDC. In the state of UP the executive committee at the district level is called 'Pariyojana Rachnavan Abayutan Samithi' which also has to arrange for institutional finance for the implementation of IRDP and other schemes. It also ensures coordination between state sector and district level schemes so as to avoid duplication of effort. The 'Core Group' in Assam at the district level is responsible for preparation of draft sub-divisional plans. It also scrutinises the operational plan submitted by the district heads of development departments. In Karnataka there are Standing Committees in finance and audit, planning and development, public works and amenities, social justice, education, agriculture and animal husbandry, health and industries. These are, in fact, executive committees. In West Bengal also there are Standing Committees at the ZP as well as Panchayat Samithi level known as "Parikalpa-o-Unnayan Asthayee Samithi". This committee undertakes resource survey and assist in formulating plan for the district at the district level and for reviewing the progress of various development plans.

District Planning Cell/Unit: The task of Executive Committee is facilitated by the Planning cell/unit at the district level. A review of the organisational structure available in district planning in different states has revealed that 17 States in the country have established Planning Cell at the district level with varying pattern and composition. In the State of Tamil Nadu in only three districts the planning cells have been constituted whereas in Rajasthan the District Planning officer is attached to DRDA. These District Planning Cells have very limited staff and in most cases consist of a Chief Planning Officer/District Planning Officer assisted by statistical and research assistants and clerical staff. The Chief Planning Officer is invariably from statistical background except in Kerala and Gujarat where officers from Indian Administrative Service and other state services are also inducted to this post. The officers in the planning cells by and large do not have any qualification in planning. Even though this is supposed to be a technical cell, the functions being discharged by this Cell are only compilation of planning proposals received from sectoral officers and rendering assistance to the District Planning Board/Committee in its routine monitoring of the process of implementation of the plan projects.

Functional Decentralisation

For operationalisation of micro planning, identification of schemes and activities to be planned and implemented at the district level and below is very crucial. This necessitates defining the scope of the micro level plan explicitly to make it clear to the planning and implementing agencies their real roles, leaving no scope for confusion and duplication in their role performance. Moreover, the quantum of fund to be earmarked for plan implementation at district level and below have also to be decided on the basis of the schemes to be taken up at these levels.

It may be noted that out of 21 states who have accepted the concept of micro level planning only 15 states have identified schemes for planning at micro level, that too differs from state to state. The states like Bihar, Gujarat, Maharashtra, Orissa, Uttar Pradesh have identified district sector schemes whereas the state of Assam has gone a step ahead in functional decentralisation and identified sub-divisional level schemes. There are also states like Madhya Pradesh and West Bengal which have listed out block level schemes whereas Andhra Pradesh and Karnataka have mandal level schemes also. In spite of this diversity, except Assam, most of the states have categorised district sector schemes. The basic principle followed in the identification of the district sector schemes is that the schemes' benefits would be confined to the district. Thus, schemes like agricultural production and minor irrigation, soil conservation, animal husbandry, forestry, horticulture, small scale industry, primary and secondary education, district and village roads, rural electrification, rural water supply and sanitation, health, rural housing, social welfare, and cooperation, etc. are of relevance to individual districts and hence are classified under district sector schemes.

Gujarat has classified the district level schemes further, based on the type of fund available for taking up the schemes at the district level and below. Thus, the schemes admissible under discretionary outlays, incentive outlays and schemes not admissible under discretionary and incentive outlays have been listed out.

Devolution of Financial Resources

The disaggregation of state plan outlays for districts and other lower units on rational basis is quite essential for making micro level planning a fruitful exercise. The State governments have realised its importance and hence accepted the basic idea of disaggregation of state plan outlay into state sector outlay and district sector outlay.

It may be observed that the division of the state plan outlays into state and district sector outlays depend upon the number of schemes listed out at these levels. In general about 30-40 per cent of the total outlay of the state plan is earmarked for district sector schemes. In Assam it is 20 per cent, Uttar Pradesh 30 per cent, Andhra Pradesh 40 per cent, Bihar, Gujarat and Kerala 40 per cent, Maharashtra and Jammu and Kashmir 40-45 per cent. The district sector outlay so arrived at is redistributed among different districts on the basis of some variants of Gadgil formula. The common criteria of the allocation formula are:

1. Total population
2. Population of SC/ST small farmers
3. Agriculture backwardness
4. Irrigation backwardness
5. Industrial backwardness
6. Communication backwardness
7. Drinking water problem
8. Others

Out of these criteria population is generally given a weightage of 50 to 60 per cent.

The outlay, thus, arrived at for each district is distributed among different sectors/sub-divisions/blocks/mandals as the case may be. In Assam 50 per cent of the district sector allocation is distributed to different sub-divisions. In Jammu and Kashmir, Kerala and West Bengal it is distributed among blocks and in Karnataka among mandals. This distribution is done on the basis of some approved norms.

Out of the district sector outlay about 80 per cent is generally reserved for the normal district level schemes approved by the State

Planning Departments and formulated as per the guidelines of the Central and State Governments. In most cases sector-wise allocation of the district fund is communicated by the State Planning Departments leaving little scope for the district level planning body to fix up sectoral priority based on the local potentialities, problems and people's need. However, in a number of states to provide some freedom to the district planning bodies some fund is kept aside to be utilised by the local agency for implementing schemes of local importance selected by them. These are: discretionary outlays or untied fund.

The amount earmarked as untied fund is as high as Rs. 3 crores per district in Bihar and in Orissa it is Rs.25-30 lakhs per district. The states like Bihar, Himachal Pradesh, and Orissa distribute the untied fund among districts on the basis of certain formulae whereas in other states lump sum amount is provided to districts under this head.

The concept of incentive outlay is in vogue in Andhra Pradesh, Gujarat and Jammu and Kashmir. The incentive outlays are allocated against some matching fund raised by the local agency for implementing schemes of their choice. In Andhra Pradesh a lump sum of Rs. 50 lakhs per district is provided as incentive outlay for the implementation of 'Telugu Grameena Kranti Patham Scheme'. In Jammu and Kashmir also the allocation under this head is same. Gujarat has a different pattern and 5 per cent of the total district sector allocation is reserved for incentive outlay and is distributed among talukas in the district on the basis of certain criteria.

Plan Formulation, Implementation and Monitoring

Currently in most of the states at the micro level, only annual action plans are prepared. Even in the States of Assam, Jammu and Kashmir and Karnataka where sub-divisions, blocks and mandals respectively have been accepted as planning units, plan formulation exercise is confined to the district level. In Andhra Pradesh where mandals have been carved out as development units, plans for agriculture, sericulture, animal husbandry, etc. are formulated at the state level and plans for other sectors are prepared by the concerned district heads of departments. In Gujarat, schemes to be implemented with the discretionary and incentive outlays are chalked out by the Taluka Planning Committees which is finalised by the District Planning Boards, whereas, planning for the normal district sector schemes are dealt with by the concerned sectoral officers at the district level. In West Bengal the district level sectoral officers also formulate plan for district level schemes, the 'Parikalpana-o-Unayan Asthayee Samithi' (block level standing committee) identifies feasible schemes for the blocks to be incorporated by the block planning committee in the block development plan.

The Annual Action Plan proposals so formulated by the sectoral officers are scrutinised at the district level by an executive body. In Assam scrutiny of plan proposals is done by a core group at the district level, in Gujarat by the Executive Planning Committee, in Karnataka by District Planning Unit, in Kerala by working groups, in Maharashtra by District Planning Unit followed by Executive Committee, as well as State Planning Department and in Orissa by working groups.

In most cases the plans approved at the district level are forwarded to Government for final approval. In Assam sub-divisional planning and development council gives plan approval. In Andhra Pradesh it is the District Planning and Review Board which approves plan. Similarly in Bihar, it is the District Planning and Development Council, in Gujarat and Jammu and Kashmir by District Planning Boards, in Karnataka by Zilla Parishad, in Kerala by District Advisory Committee for SC (only special component plan), in Madhya Pradesh by District Planning Boards, in Maharashtra by District Planning and Development Council, in Orissa by District Planning Board, in Uttar Pradesh by District Planning and Monitoring Committee, and in West Bengal by District Planning Committee. In the case of Karnataka, Zilla Parishad is vested with powers to accord final sanction.

The plan formulation exercise generally starts in the latter half of the year. The draft plan is submitted by the sectoral officers to the district level authorities within two months. In Bihar, plan formulation commences in the month of August/September.

As regards implementation of the plan schemes, it is invariably undertaken by the district level departments, as per the guidelines and directions received from the State headquarters. In Andhra Pradesh the beneficiary oriented programmes and schemes of different agencies and corporations are implemented through Mandal Praja Parishad. In Karnataka the plan is implemented by the sectoral officers at the district level with the help of Mandal level officers. All the activities of the Zilla Parishad are implemented through nine standing committees. In Madhya Pradesh Janapath Panchayats are responsible for the implementation of certain schemes related to Agriculture, Forestry,

Animal Husbandry, Public Works, Engineering Education, Social Welfare and Cooperation. The implementation of these schemes are taken up by the concerned departments.

The progress of implementation of the plan schemes are monitored at different levels. In Assam monthly meetings of district development body are held for monitoring as well as to ensure interdepartmental coordination in plan implementation. Even the sub-divisional planning and development council is required to monitor the progress of implementation at least twice a year. In Andhra Pradesh District Development and Review Board monitors the plan implementation. In Bihar, the implementation of Annual Action Plan is discussed in the monthly meetings of the DPDC and the departments are also required to furnish their monthly progress reports. In Gujarat the District Planning Board monitors progress of implementation of Minimum Needs and Poverty Alleviation Programmes. Executive Planning Committee, District Planning Officer as well as State Planning Department also monitor the progress of plan execution in this state.

In Himachal Pradesh the State government has fixed norms for utilisation of funds under the plan scheme for each quarter of the financial year. The progress reports of financial and physical content of plan schemes are reviewed in the quarterly meetings of the District Planning and Development Committee. In Jammu and Kashmir review of implementation of Annual Plans is done by the state cabinets along with sectoral officers in the districts. In Karnataka monitoring and review of the development activities are taken up by different departments, mandals and planning units. The progress reports received by the planning units are placed in the Zilla Parishad monthly review meetings. In Kerala the implementation of Special Component Plan is reviewed by the District Advisory Committee for SCs and other programmes by the District Development Council. In Maharashtra, regular reviews of the implementation of plan programmes at the district level is ensured through monthly meetings of the executive committee of the district planning and development council.

Thus, it can be seen that micro level planning is only a periodical exercise and by and large perspective plans are not drawn up. The plan formulation is undertaken by the sectoral departments and compiled by the Executive Planning Committees or district planning units and placed in the district planning boards. The plan implementation is undertaken through the respective departments under the guidance of heads of departments except some of the beneficiary-oriented and employment generation schemes which are implemented at the taluka/block/mandal levels. Monitoring of implementation of schemes is undertaken through periodical review meetings held under the auspices of District Planning and Development Boards with the exception of Karnataka where it is reviewed by Zilla Parishad and in Jammu and Kashmir by the State Cabinet in addition to the regular reviews in the District Development Board. Nevertheless, a project approach and an in built system for periodical monitoring and applying corrective measures is lacking in the micro level plans formulated by almost all the States.

The history of planning since independence in the country is adorned by several bold experiments. Micro level planning is one among the many in the list. Nevertheless, it is heartening to note that 21 States in the country have accepted this concept and have constituted district level advisory bodies. Out of these states 17 have gone one step ahead and have also established district planning cells.

The fact cannot be denied that it is a major achievement and it is evident that the stage is set in these states, for formulation of micro level plans, but one point which has to be also borne in mind is the poor capability of the agency or the existing set up to handle this technical task of planning. As a micro level plan is required to respond to the local problems, to take care of the local requirements, and also make proper use of the available limited resources through productive processes, the exercise of planning at this level is a complicated and a challenging exercise. It was assessed as early as in 1977 by Prof. Dantwala that there is hardly any skill available at the block level for micro level planning. The situation has not improved much since then, and it will not be an exaggeration to say that the technical know-how or skill for plan formulation is yet to percolate below the state level in most of the cases. It was envisaged that the district planning team will formulate Perspective and Annual Action Plan for the area but in practice this task is not attended to by any district planning team in the country. The main function of this team is to collect the plans prepared by the sectoral officers, compile it, examine it against the financial allocations made for these sectors and schemes and also to collect the plans prepared by the sectoral officers, compile it, examine it against the financial allocations made for these sectors and schemes and also to collect the progress report from the implementing agencies. Thus, the planning team is meant only for non planning work, and the expectation that the formulation of scientific micro level plans will be facilitated by establishing the planning team so constituted is a myth.

In spite of these organisational arrangements, still it is the sectoral officers who are responsible for chalking out the plan schemes on the basis of the guidelines received from the State Planning Department or Heads of Departments as well as the fund available for their sectors. The database required for plan formulation available with these officers are inadequate and the officer concerned has no choice but to go by his subjective judgement and past experience. In the absence of detailed area/location-wise information on resource potentiality of different sectors, the officers are not in a position to go beyond listing out of schemes irrespective of their feasibility, and just indicate the financial requirements of these schemes. Moreover, the locations at which these schemes can be taken up on priority basis do not form part of the plan. Thus, the plan so prepared is devoid of the spatial feature which is an important component of micro level plan. These plans also do not reflect the felt need of the people.

The plan proposals, thus, arrived at are just compiled as a comprehensive plan and placed before the District Planning Body for approval. It is at this stage that the people's participation in planning through peoples' representatives (who are supposed to be people's spokesmen) is ensured. As a ritual some suggestions are made at this stage and some minor modifications are also made. The plan is then reviewed at the state level and undergoes some pruning keeping in view the financial constraints. Thus, the prevalent system is not conducive for producing "micro level plan". It is a plan fórmulated in isolation by the sectoral officers on the basis of the guidelines worked out at the state level within the financial ceiling indicated, without peoples participation, ignoring integrated planning approach and also omitting spatial allocation of resources.

The review of the current-status of micro level planning in the country pin-points the need to take up the following measures for projecting micro level planning in the country. These are:

Improved Database

In order to formulate realistic plans on scientific lines at the micro level, the first pre-requisite is strengthening of database. To start with, socio-economic information should be gathered and maintained adopting village as the basic unit. The natural resource inventory showing the distribution pattern level of utilisation along with potentiality for future development is essential for identification of schemes.

Strengthening of Planning Cell

As the sectoral proposals are drawn in isolation by the officers of concerned departments it is necessary that these proposals are properly re-examined and integrated to make them realistic and derive optimum return from these schemes. This necessitates deployment of officers trained in Regional Planning/Area Planning in the Planning Cells to perform this task in an efficient way.

The second important role of the District Planning Cell would be formulation of "Spatial Plan" to translate the socio-economic plan into location specific action plans. The spatial plan is also a tool for physical integration of different schemes. As there is no sectoral department to deal with this aspect, the District Planning Cell has to take care of it. This is a specialised job and would require the services of a trained planner. It is in this context that the Planning Commission has suggested a spatial planner as a member of the planning team which need to appointed on priority basis.

Training of Sectoral Officers

The sectoral officers will continue to be the main instrument for project identification even after strengthening the district planning cell. Hence, in order to improve the quality of plan formulation, the sectoral officers need to be trained in the methods and techniques of plan formulation. Their training should have two components. First they should be exposed to the aspects of comprehensive development plan like concept, components and steps. The second part of the training should be on plan formulation for the concerned sectors.

Formulation of Perspective Development Plan

By and large, currently planning process is limited to formulation of annual action plans. But for determining the scope of development in different sectors and to fix up the priority of implementation of different schemes a perspective development plan reflecting resource potential of the area is a basic requirement. This will facilitate to foresee the requirements of different activities and areas and enable to take advance action to meet these requirements.

potentiality for future development is essential for identification of schemes.

Strengthening of Planning Cell

As the sectoral proposals are drawn in isolation by the offices of concerned departments it is necessary that these proposals are programmed and integrated to make them realistic and derive optimum return from these schemes. This necessitates deployment of officers trained in Regional Planning/Area Planning in the Planning Cell to perform this task in an efficient way.

The second important role of the District Planning Cell would be formulation of "Spatial Plan" to translate the socio-economic plan into location specific action plans. The spatial plan is also a tool for physical integration of different schemes. As there is no sectoral department to deal with this aspect, the District Planning Cell has to take care of it. This is a specialised job and would require the services of a trained planner. It is in this context that the Planning Commission has suggested a spatial planner as a member of the planning team which need be appointed on priority basis.

Training of Sectoral Officers

The sectoral officers will continue to be the main instruments for project identification even after strengthening the district planning cell. Hence, in order to improve the quality of plan formulation, the sectoral officers need to be trained in the methods and techniques of plan formulation. Their training should have two components. First, they should be exposed to the aspects of comprehensive development plan like concept, components and steps. The second part of the training should be on plan formulation for the concerned sectors.

Formulation of Perspective Development Plan

By and large, currently planning process is limited to formulation of annual Action Plans. But for determining the scope of development in different sectors and to fix up the priority of implementation of different schemes a perspective development plan reflecting resource potential of the area is a basic requirement. This will facilitate to foresee the requirements of different activities and areas and enable to take advance action to meet these requirements.

5

DECENTRALISED PLANNING, APPREHENSIONS AND ENVIRONMENT: An Analytical Framework

Amitava Mukherjee

The scenerio of decentralised planning at the district and sub-district levels or micro-level planning as Thaha calls them (see the foregoing paper), foregoing, may reflect several things to different people: it may reflect lack of political will, lack of bureaucratic will, paucity of foresight, half hearted attempts, reluctance to share power and so on. Though some or all the these may or may not be true, under-lying all this failure to establish a system of decentralised multi-level planning despite nearly three decades of "struggle" to do so, is a certain basket of apprehension, which in lesser or greater measure has influenced our initiative to decentralize, yet curiously enough these apprehensions never encompassed an apprehension about how a non-decentralised planning system (I deliberately avoid using the word "Centralised") has endangered our environmental balance. In this paper therefore, I propose to deal, in the main, with apprehensions about decentralised planning, some real and some "virtual", and a non-apprehension about non-decentralised planning.

Many doubts have been entertained and apprehensions held out about the implications of decentralisation and decentralised planning in India. That is an attitude of mind which is understandable because of the uncharted nature of territory ahead; because of the fear of the unknown and because of the compunctions involved in shedding powers from the bureaucracy, political citadel and centralised governance. The fears are, however, not well founded and in some instances even exaggerated, and in any event, the probable problems, real and imaginary were not intractable, for Man's will has always solved the seemingly unsolvable and the drama of Man's march from barbarianism to civilisation is nothing but the drama of Man's success and failure at solving the problems that confront him.

The power-status structure of society is of crucial importance,[1] because many of the apprehensions about decentralised planning revolve around the pivot of local power-status structure. The exploitative role of the local-power-status structure over the ages to promote their own narrow parochial, and personal sectoral interests, their near limitless capacity to appropriate bounties offered by Fiscal Policy and their proverbial indifference towards the needs, entitlements and deprivation of the weaker sections of the rural society have all made an already difficult situation still worse. Yet these general statements may not always turn out to be true for at least two good reasons: One, the strength of the local power-status-structure is not uniform throughout the country and indeed they exhibit wide variations in the effective power that local power-status-structure can wield because India itself is not a homogenous country in terms of customs, practice, usage, value system, morals and income level; two, the constituents of the local power-status-structure are heterogeneous and a divergence of the interests of different constituents of the same local power-status structure are so widespread that they may not always be able to act in perfect unison, even when they wanted to, as a cohesive force perpetrating poverty on the rural poor perpetually. The non-homogeneous character in local power-status-structure can unleash divergent and opposing forces, which in the ultimate analysis can offset each other, and their net effects virtually neutralised.

Assuming that the local power-status structure is capable of perpetrating poverty on the rural poor, nevertheless the decentralised planning system, does have effective mechanisms within itself to check, if not totally circumvent, the negative consequences of the local level power-status-structure. The existence of multiple inter-related tiers of local government itself provides one such mechanism and within each tier of local government, like the Gram Panchayats, the interface between the decision-makers and the affected sections of the population scales down considerably the role of local power-status-structure. Accountability of the elected representatives who are the decision-makers, to the people on whose behalf they take decisions, can be ensured by mandatory elections of local level organisations, like Gram Panchayats at given intervals as enjoined in the earlier Panchayati Raj Bill defeated in the Parliament and in the latter version of it recently approved by the Parliament and by fighting these elections along political lines following the West-Bengal model. Consequently, while the possible negative consequences of the local-level power-status-structure, could continue to be a cause for concern, it is nonetheless not an intractable problem because of the existing built-in checks and balances in a system of decentralised governance, decentralised planning and development efforts, and because of additional checks that can be built in through executive fiats or legislative measures for protecting the neglected, poorer and weaker sections of society.

While it is undeniable that local-level conflicts, grounded in well-entrenched patterns of social and economic stratification, are said to restrict seriously the domain of community action essential for the success, to its freest extent, of decentralised development, this may not always be necessarily true, because it is indeed arguable that socio-economic conflicts are intense precisely because of the stagnant rural society with expanding disparities, where a few gain, most do not and many lose. With decision-making nearer to the scene of action, with the affected people in a decentralised system of governance and decentralised planning set up, nearer to decision-makers, an initial impetus to the economic activities that raise the productivity of rural resources, in some favourably placed areas, would act as the "premium mobile" for development of an area and its adjoining periphery,[2] which can act as a healthy "demonstration effect" to be consolidated through quick dissemination of information about the progress of adjoining regions. All this would induce a chain of multiplier effects to set in, over a period of time, resulting in a widening and deepening of collective local action necessary to extract the full mileage out of the available growth opportunities to conform to the principle of the "greatest good of the greatest number". Such dynamic growth impulse can only focus attention on developmental efforts as an alternate to the stagnation-induced socio-economic conflicts.

Much is made about the eventuality that the local level power-status-structure with all its hostility (expressed and latent) towards the interests of the poor and weaker sections of society, would be iniquitous, and the underlying premises is that the elected functionaries and the bureaucracy far removed from the pulls and pressures of the local level power-status-structure are freer to act in the best interest of the poor for the benefit of a wider cross-section of the poorer and weaker segments of society. This on the face of, is specious in the context of a decentralised governance and decentralised planning set up, because the decentralised institutions provide the mechanism to build enforceable checks that contain the negative forces of local level power-status-structure within tolerable limits. The periodic elections (fought along political lines) to the Gram Panchayats and Zilla Parishads or other variants of Panchayati Raj Institutions, according to an enacted law and the reservation of appropriate seats in such Panchayati Raj Institutions for the women and the weaker sections of society would lend a voice to the less visible and less articulate sections of the vast mass of rural community. In the short and long-runs, the development of these forces and possibilities which they would open up, will be in themselves the required guarantee for imparting the development process a pro-poor tilt as has happened, to a large extent, in the West Bengal experiment. A continued reliance on a remote controlled centralised system of administration and of developmental efforts, can never tilt the development process in favour of the poor, as evidenced by forty years of our planning effort, which can be best summarised as "experimentations at centralisation".

The content of decentralised development may not at times, it has been so believed for long, conform to the overall national and state plan priorities given the federal structure of our country. However, this need not be so because after all, the spheres and the focus of each tier of development planning and effort will be clearly earmarked,[3] with only local activities like basic amenities and better harnessing of the production potential of local resources need be invested at the district level schemes, and activities that cut across districts but within states are assigned for State level planning and schemes and activities that cut across States or in which either States and districts may not be interested in or may not have the resources to undertake, are earmarked as the exclusive preserve for national level action. In the West Bengal decentralised planning system, even the schemes at the village level are identified, and schemes which cannot be included in the village level schemes but are essential for a village or group of villages, are included in the Gram Panchayat Plans. And schemes which cannot be included in the Gram Panchayat Plans but are deemed important for the Panchayats, are included in the Block Level Plan. The schemes, programmes and plans are clearly laid down. If this clear demarcation of developmental activities (one of the principles of decentralised planning) which is essential and which deserves high priority in our scheme for decentralised planning is adhered to, the possibility of the content of decentralised planning not conforming to National and State priorities is remote. In any event, additional safeguards could be built into the scheme of transfer of functions and resources to lower level developmental agencies to correct any significant distortion that could creep in. A classic example in point is the Jawahar Rojgar Yojana for poverty alleviation. Though the funds flowed from the Centre, the implementation of the scheme was entrusted totally to the Gram Panchayats, with guidelines about the details of appropriation, allocation and spacing of doses, and the scheme despite all the criticisms levelled against it has worked very well because the people generally owned up the activities, considered them as their own.[4] My personal discussion with many villagers in the hills of U.P. and Bihar, and in West Bengal has revealed that the people (the sample may be small and hence open to attack) unanimously feel that the scheme would have worked much better had it been implemented four decades ago, when people were less impatient, when their hopes were not yet belied and when their vision of a beautiful India was still shinning. We are late.

And then, let it be clearly recognised that distortions in development priorities have been, to a large extent, the outcome of the centralised planning system itself and often involving huge investments in some pockets which have failed to promote the professed equity in the distribution of wealth and income, and increases in productivity which were intended to make prosperity an all pervading phenomenon. For the success of our development endeavours we need to enrich them with the creativity, innovations and ideas of the millions of people, for whose benefit the development process in designed. The participatory process itself, inherent in a decentralised system, stimulates the contribution and creativity of the people, and that clearly is a leap forward in developmental planning efforts because unless the people participate in the adventure of development, the development forces cannot be all pervasive and long lasting.[5]

There are apprehensions relating to the availability of planning and administrative expertise at district and sub-district levels, on account of several causes. Firstly, there has been an under-estimation of local-level knowledge of local conditions, local resources, local-level problems. The existing developmental super-structure, arrangements, schemes and even programmes tend to be grounded on a set standard format that is "inelastic" to regional variations in as diverse a country as India, assuming that decision-makers far removed from the scene of action, are capable of having most unorthodox objective view of the community of resources and community of people, where those resources will be set to operate upon.[6] If the local level institutions are left to decide for themselves the appropriateness of developmental efforts in their context and have the liberty to chart out the destination and distribution of resources, the likelihood of better correlation between the programmes content and the local problems and possibilities, comprehensively brightens up. In any event, the expertise available with the bureaucracy will be at the disposal of the local institutions, and as I have argued elsewhere, the people who will be put in charge of framing, implementing and monitoring decentralised planning will have to be appropriately trained and equipped of which providing a manual for preparing plans at the district and sub-district levels is essential.[7] The deficiencies that would still persist can be circumvented to a large extent if the national and State level agencies provide the supportive role in providing information on resources, opportunities opened up by extra-local investments and technical expertise, and the deficiencies that would continue to haunt the process even then would be eliminated with the process proceeding itself through experience, experimentation and extension.[8]

The local level functionaries involved in the decentralisation of decision-making for local level planning and developmental efforts, can draw upon the expertise available locally in the large body of educational, technical, economic, social and voluntary institutions and other professional bodies that are located in the local region, whose systematic involvement would help the decentralised bodies in the formulation and implementation of good and comprehensive area development plans. The formation of the Agro-climatic Local Teams headed by the Vice-Chancellor of an Agricultural University falling within the Zone, have been operationalised on this principle, and some of the plans prepared in the districts, such as the one in Mysore,[9] place a whole lot of reliance on this interweaving of the ideas and efforts of a wide cross-section of the local people. These efforts also impart a sense of belonging to the local intelligentsia and opinion leaders in the planning process whose participation is crucial to the success of decentralisation, because in addition to their providing locally available expertise in the formulation of the local plans, these men and women will have their own outlook broadened and favourably disposed towards decentralisation and decentralised planning, by their interface with the local people's representatives, by their way of posing the local-level problems, and by having a closer look at the picture of poverty and deprivation that afflicts most of the local populace which they might not have perceived in their humdrum lives. Populist demands and excessive demands on financial resources can be considerably sobered by a budget constraint to the extent that resources devolving from the state to the local bodies will be in terms of a set criteria, and some such criteria indeed exists for most States for the present howsoever rudimentary they may be,[10] but these are by no means sacrosant and they can well be reviewed, rationalised and modified by setting up State Finance Commissions, who would also decide upon the quantum or resources to be made available to the decentralised and local bodies. Attention is invited to the *Recommendations*, of the International Expert Group Meeting on *Decentralised Planning*, held at the Lal Bahadur Shastri National Academy of Administration, (Government of India) Mussoorie for 11th to 13th June, 1990. It would clearly be possible to enjoin that any additional devolution of resources should aim at encouraging community action and mobilisation, conservation and efficient use of physical and financial resources available locally, and efficiency in use of natural resources tempered by environmental considerations. The Gujarat experiment at encouraging local resources is a good beginning though admittedly a lot remains to be done.[11] There is no reason to believe that in the hands of the decentralised bodies, *prima facie*, the resources available under the currently centrally-administered programmes, like JRY, cannot be more effectively utilised, and indeed the first experiment through JRY has been successful in this regard (as mentioned earlier) at least to the extent that in many villages in the Garhwal Hill, of which I have personal knowledge, this was the first time that any money for development purposes have come about and people have, in many villages at least, participated in the programme with a sense of belonging and modest pride. The leakages of funds about which so much is spoken and written about, as mentioned earlier can be reduced by encouraging selection of activities (through local level participation) that provide more durable means of income and working to the poor and by ensuring the supporting investments which are not visibly substantial as of now. It may be reiterated here, even at the cost of suffering the stricture of being repetitive, that in any event none can vouch that leakages do not occur as much or as little, when schemes are implemented from above, by the State level or Central Government or their agencies.

What is Local Planning All About

The philosophy of decentralised planning is that there exists a wide canvas of developmental activity in which local people, local institutions and local governance are better positioned *vis-a-vis* the central planners to adapt programmes to the specific requirements of particular villages, panchayats, blocks or districts. As decentralisation of planned activities is introduced and progressively increased, an eruption of charters of demands would be the rule, and naturally so, because the general mass would seek to redress all their problems with which they have struggled far too long to have any more patience. However, with development proceeding along lines, which is perceived by the local people and their representatives as being high on their priority list, and as their understanding that the available resources are limited *vis-a-vis* their unlimited needs, the clamour for indiscriminate demands for development will give way to an appreciation of the need to tackle the problems systematically on a long term basis instead of the mad rush for short-run gains. The scheme of priority for any such exercise would be:

(a) ensuring accessibility of the people to needs of nutrition, primary health, education, drinking water, housing, sanitation, availability of public distribution system and other essential social amenities within the perspective period chosen;

(b) providing local roads, rural electrification, credit and marketing facilities, and other economic infrastructure; and

(c) providing for programmes for augmenting production and employment in the region, be it the village, the gram panchayat, the block or the district.

These have been discussed at several places and we, therefore, need not discuss them in detail here. What, however, has not received adequate emphasis is the issues appertaining to resource planning. It has to be clearly understood that the critical value of water, energy and biomass (in the form of trees) occupy a central place in a decentralised planning process. The typical approach to resource planning in the past has been to project future demand for these resources, based on past trends, and arrange for providing an increased supply of the natural resources to meet the growing demand, an approach that clearly suffered from three infirmities: *one*, it did not consider it expedient to take stock of the available stock of these resources; *two*, the structure and benefits of demand and the efficiency in the use of resources was kept out of the picture; and *three*, the issues pertaining to attempts at replenishing these resources, to the extent possible was never tackled - systematically, barring few *ad hoc* exceptions. This is best illustrated by reference to agriculture, which continues to sustain a greater part of our population.

TABLE 5.1: Growth Rates in Resource Use in Indian Agriculture (Roy *et al.*, 1979)

	1951-56	1956-61	1951-61	1961-66	1966-71	1961-71
Land						
Net Sown Area[1]	1.88	0.73	1.30	0.48	0.35	1.42
Arable land area[1]	5.22	0.15	2.66	0.61	0.15	1.76
Gross Sown Area[1]	2.22	0.97	1.59	0.40	0.91	1.66
Net Irrigated Area[1]	1.66	1.77	1.72	1.68	3.12	2.40
Gross Irrigated Area[1]	2.49	1.91	2.10	2.38	3.94	3.16
Cropping intensity	0.35	0.17	0.26	0.00	0.52	1.26
Human and Bullock Labour						
Work Force in Agriculture[2]	-	-	3.02	-	-	2.02
Rural Population[2]	-	-	2.01	-	-	2.02
Draft Animals[2]	0.96	1.98	1.47	0.14	0.34	0.25
Fertilizer						
Fertilizer consumption (NPK)[1]	18.47	18.71	18.59	21.39	21.46	21.42
Capital Investment						
Oil engine pumps[3]	8.45	15.81	12.07	13.46	27.03	20.24
Electric Pumps[3]	10.76	26.19	18.22	20.70	31.27	25.98
Tractors[3]	19.44	8.11	13.64	11.73	21.05	16.72

Sources: (1) *Statistical Abstract*, India, (2) *Draft Five Year Plan: 1978-83*, (3) *Fertilizer Statistics*.

Notes: [1]Computed between centred 3-year average of 1950-52, 1955-57, 1960-62, 1965-77 and 1970-72.

[2]Computed between the adjusted population census years data of 1951, 1961, and 1971.

[3]Computed between the livestock census years of 1951, 1956, 1961, 1966, and 1972.

In the initial years of our experimentation with planned economic development, population explosion had increased the demand for foodgrains and at once increased the supply of able bodied agricultural workforce as an input for stepping up agricultural activity. With virtually no improvement in technology, extension of cultivation to meet increased demand for foodgrain followed. As a result the growth rate of net sown area was to the tune of 1.30 per cent per annum during 1951-61 as against 0.42 per cent between 1961-71. The growth rate of arable land area was 2.66 per cent between 1951-61 as against 0.76 between 1961-71. That agricultural growth was brought about by "extensive cultivation" is further borne by the fact that between 1951-56, growth rate in cropping intensity was 0.35 per cent; between 1956-61, it dropped to 0.17 per cent and between 1961-66 it dropped further 0.00 per cent.[12] Encroachment of common land and forests to bring them under cultivation followed as natural corollary,[13] which accounts for nearly 50 per cent of the forest cover destroyed so far. Between 1951-52 and 1975-76, out of 4.41 million hectare of forest cover destroyed, as high as 2.51 million hectares has been on account of extension in agriculture.

This extension is the area under cultivation was accompained by an increase in the cattle population, required for the increased area to be cultivated. Several studies, amongst which Vaidyanathan (1988), in a prominent one, have comprehensively established this point. The growth rate in draft animals was 0.96 per cent between 1951-56 and 1.98 per cent between 1956-61 (this dropped to 0.25% between 1961-71, and between 1961-66 it was even as low as 0.14%), which exerted pressure on grazing land and pastures, and with common lands brought under the plough, the pressure of grazing extended on the depleted, or depleting, forest land, causing soil erosion and eco-degradation on a very substantial scale. Thus eco-degradation and natural resource depletion are consequences of the failure of our centrally administered plans to cope with increased demand for food and fodder (and fuel wood and other forest produce as well) through necessary investments, technological changes and institutional arrangements at ground conditions.

After the introduction of technological change in agriculture from the late sixties, pressure on common land and forests for agriculture came down but labour-absorption did not increase as many studies like Rao, Ray & Subbarao (1988) have established or, as A.K. Sen wrote, the investments in agriculture has been "landesque" and not "labouresque". And in a majority of the States (baring Andhra Pradesh, Haryana, Punjab and Western U.P.) growth in agricultural output was less than the growth in population, or in terms of the outdated Malthusian terminology, the growth in population outstripped growth in subsistence (even after deleting the juxtoposition of the arithmetic and geometric progression rates), as a result of which poverty persisted, and the bulk of the poor were agricultural labourers, who remained idle for nearly six months in a year. The pressure on natural resources persisted : since prices of fuel and wood increased several fold in urban and semi-urban areas, cutting the forest became an attractive source of income for the rural poor, at times financed and protected by unscrupulous contractors and intermediaries. Here the poor household partook the nature of a monopoly firm without a marginal cost curve because of the reasons that:

(i) the poor household was without employment and so it was putting in its labour which was free and even without a transfer price;
(ii) no other variable factor input was required (including zero transportation cost as the poor household would lug the timber;
(iii) and the capital input, reflecting fixed cost was almost negligible.

Thus felling the forest continued till the marginal revenue curve intersected the horizontally axis, where total revenue, and hence, total profits were maximised as shown in Fig. 5.1. The impact on forests, tantamounted to a rampage of natural resources.

Under a system of decentralised planning, this reckless use of (or mis-use of) resources is expected to be reduced. Forest and common property resources would come under community management through what is called "collective vigilance". The control and management of all government land within a village be transferred to individual settlements (may be Gram Sabha) so that each village has a clearly demarcated environment to protect, develop and use. No individual can encroach common property resources for his individual well-being by causing injury to community interest, which would bring greater gains to each individual acting collectively than under unbridled exploitation of natural resources severally. This has indeed been in operation in some villages in South India as investigated by Robert Wade.[14] Wade found that there are community enforced rules for water distribution and animal grazing. "Farmers who try to interfere with water allocations are liable to be reported to the village council and made to pay a fine. During a drought . . . the fines may run up to Rs.20 to Rs.50 per offence. But the main penalty is the loss of reputation when the offender is dressed down in front of the council and the onlookers".[15] When animals are caught grazing a standing crop, they are taken to the pound, and a fine of Rs. 2 during day and Rs. 4 during night is imposed where the number of animals is small. If the number of animals is large the council decides on the merits of each case and the fine can run into hundreds of rupees.

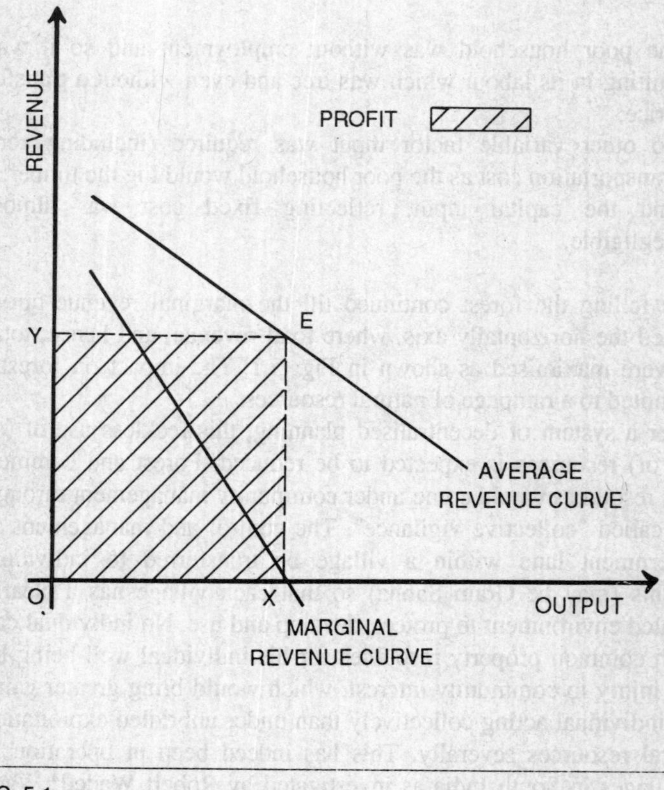

FIG. 5.1

The main hurdle to community management of the foregoing variety is the big-landowner-moneylender-contractor-petty-bureaucrat nexus, which can be broken only if the people are organised for a common cause around the pivot of decentralised planning. "Development of Organisational Capacity" for the common man to "participate in the management of common resources should ensure for them a continuous role in the planning, operating and maintenance of the common system so that it would not lapse back to its unproductive condition".[16] And indeed planned efforts of the Government of India at environmental protection administered from New Delhi is doomed to failure because of the diversity of India's land mass and human mass. Because of the diversity in India's landmass and human mass, environmental protection and development can be made sustainable only if these programmes are conceived, planned and implemented at the grassroots level where these can indeed be eco-system specific, involving the common people wholly. For the common man to actively operate for eco-development, all rural settlements must be endowed with an active institution (like the Panchayats) which has legal control over its immediate environment and access to resources, either as levies, grants or loans.

The typical traditional approach to resource planning (not in line with the foregoing) has not merely caused a wastage of resources and damage to the environment but has caused poverty to spread, man-power to be wasted and has accelerated the pace of migration of rural labour to urban metropolises, adding to their distress in no uncertain terms. As resources got depleted, the sources of water, fuel and fodder receded away from the rural habitats, and the women who have traditionally taken upon themselves the responsibility of fetching these for their household, spent a good deal of their time and energy in securing these for the upkeep of their families. This had two-fold effects: *one*, they had lesser time to tend their yards and livestock and share the burden of cultivation with their men folk, and *two*, they burnt themselves out (on an average some women walk even 8 kilometres a day to fetch fuel and drinking water) causing damage to general health. It has been estimated that as high as 40 per cent of their time is spent in collecting fuelwood alone. To be precise women in village Pakh gather 1.74 townes of firewood per annum, each firewood gethering household spends an average of 2.51 hours per day; makes 172 trips in a year and each round trip is about 8.54 kilometres in distance. In Dwing village in Uttar Pradesh, each household spends about 7.2 hours on an everage per day to search for fuel and fodder.[17] Table 5.2 is a summary of findings of several studies on these issues.

TABLE 5.2: Time taken and Distance Travelled for Firewood Collection by Region (Bina Agarwal, 1989)

Region	Years of data	Firewood Collection*		Data source
		Time taken	Distance travelled	
Chamoli (hills)		5 hr/day+	over 5 km	Swaminathan (1984)
(a) Dwing	1982	4 hr/day	over 3 km	
(b) Pakhi				
Gujarat (plains)		Once every 4 days	N.A.	Nagbrahman and Sambrani (1983)
(a) Forested	1980	Once every 2 days	4.5 km	
(b) Depleted				
(c) Severely		4-5 hr/day	N.A.	
Madhya Pradesh (plains)	1980	1-2 times/week	5 km	Chand and Bezboruah (1980)
Kumaun (hill)	1982	3 days/week	5-7 km	Floger and Dewan (1983)
Karnataka (plains)	N.A.	1 hr/day	5.4 km/trip	Batliwala (1983)
Garhwal (hill)	N.A.	5 hr/day	10 km	Agarwal (1983)
Bihar (plains)	c. 1972	N.A.	1-2 km/day	Bhaduri and Sarin (1980)
	1980	N.A.	8-10 km/day	
Rajasthan (plains)	1986 (winter)	5 hr/day	4 km	Personal observation

Notes: * Collected primarily or sorely by women and children.
+ Average computed from information given in the study.
N.A. = Information not available.

These, *inter alia*, have been contributory factors in reducing productivity and output, deepening the poverty that already afflicted the rural masses. Additionally, the receding of the bio-mass (in the form of trees) accelerated the pace of eroding the top-soil of their fields, leading to hastening the process of fall in productivity. This cycle of action and inter-action, continued till the "net product" available to a wide section of the rural mass turned insufficient to sustain them and their families, which provided the necessary condition for the migration of rural people to the urban agglomerations. We need not labour the ensuing consequence of the process which is obvious.

The infirmities mentioned above, amongst themselves, additionally were contributory factors in damaging the environment on the one hand and in causing a mounting demand for more fiscal resources to claim natural resources in even greater quantity on the other. A stage has been reached where environmental degradation has reached crisis proportions, and fiscal resources have become scarce which leaves the demand for these resources unfulfilled, because as the scarcity of natural resources successively increases, successively larger quantum of fiscal resources are required to maintain the supply of natural resources at the existing level.

Even at the great Marx who was so concerned with resources in the modern sense of the term, committed the same mistake. Marx assumed that the depletion of the existing stock of means of production (resources) is continually made good by current labour, but he scarcely realised that some depletion in means of production, in particular that of minerals, oil and coal, and bio-mass in the form of trees can never be made good by current labour.[18] The increase in productivity that comes about with technical change is by and large caused by use of energy to supplement human work, and sources of energy like coal and oil are being used up by both socialist and capitalist economies at a prodigious rate. Public opinion in the developed West has come to recognise that their economies waste energy excessively, with energy consumption having a positive correlationship with per capita income.[19] Thus for an underdeveloped country like India development along western prototype, we have been following so long, is out of the question.

Even at the cost of being repetitive, we wish to emphasize that an alternative approach to planning, therefore, as a substitute for the conventional approach is urgently required, which new approach would have, *inter alia*, three distinguishing components : *one*, the structure and management of demand for natural resources should be clearly examined; *two*, the end-use of the resources has to be ensured along the warranted path; and *three*, the efficiency of the end-use must be pitched at a very high water mark.

The demand for resources has to be estimated, not from an extrapolation of past trends, but from the perspective of uses of resources for developmental activities. Because the demands for resources in the past was never grounded essentially, upon the foundation of desired end use, such demand embodies a large element of wastage factor, which is no longer either expedient or affordable, and, therefore, extrapolation of past trends into the future would essentially mean projection of demand, based on wastage which is no longer affordable.

Thus, the emphasis in demand for resources should be based on the services that the resources would provide to the community, and how much services to provide would be a function of both quantum of resources injected into the system and the efficiency with which resources are utilised and wastages eliminated. It, therefore, follows almost axiomatically that a comparison of costs, gestation period and environment impact analysis (E.I.A.) with efficient use of resources must be made in every case which entails the use of water, energy and biomass. Experience has demonstrated that quicker and environmentally less damaging use of resources efficiently, is economically more expedient than causing incremental variations in resource supplies to sustain inefficient modes of resource utilisation. Since such comparisons are aids at decision-making, they must be made in the use of both renewable and non-renewable resources. Before leaving the context, let it be mentioned that large scale projects for resource extraction, invariably the outgrowth of centralised planning decision, ought to be weighed against small-scale extraction of resources, with regard to any form of resources, namely, water, energy or tree biomass. Thus, the area plans (what ever the delineation of the territory - villages, gram panchayats, blocks or districts) can be instruments for meeting the minimum needs of local development and at once, for the integrated development of water, land and energy, and bio-mass which is particularly important because the rapid surge of events in the foreseeable future will lead us to the situation where the village, Gram Panchayat, Block and District Plans would be cornerstones on which the arch of the State Plans would rest.[20]

Some Preemptions

This resort to decentralised planning for preservation of natural resources should not lead to the presumption that we are advocating the old and traditional methods. We do not also endorse the view that whatever is traditional and old was environmentally safe. Here resort to people's participation in conserving (and to the extent possible renewing) natural resources and environment through decentralised planning, is a strategy for eco-development, combining resource development with growth in income and alleviation of poverty on a sustainable basis.

The principal cause for substituting the traditional practices by so called new technology, is commercialisation. The gradual diminition of subsistence agriculture and the concurrent rise of commercial agriculture have radically changed the attitude of the rural masses towards use and management of natural resources, making the people protect, promote and preserve individual interest even at the expense of community goals. This is best illustrated by resort to the example of farm forestry.

Several State Government encouraged farm forestry for relieving pressure on forest, and seedlings of various species were distributed, which included eucalyptus. It is estimated that in one acre of land about 1000 trees can be planted at a spacing of 2m x 2m, insofar as eucalyptus is concerned. The farmers expect to sell each tree at around Rs.100 a piece after a gestation of seven years. Assuming as high as 50 per cent mortality rate (it normally is 20 per cent) the farmers can earn about Rs. 600 per month per acre for the next seven years.[21] Thus more and more acres are being cultivated for eucalyptus farming. As of 1985, eucalyptus farming occupied 40,000 hectares in Haryana, 1,50,000 hectares in Maharashtra, 82,000 hectares in Uttar Pradesh and 10,33,000 hectares in Karnataka.[22] The demand for eucalyptus seedling was so acute that other species had no demand so much so that 5 million seedlings of other varieties perished in the nurseries.[23]

The objectives of farm-forestry were:

(a) provision of food and fodder to forest dependent people;
(b) reduce pressure on forests and
(c) utilisation of unused farm land through (a) and (b) above.

This business of farm forestry through eucalyptus has beaten down all three since:

(i) eucalyptus is fast growing but has little to offer as fodder and the leaves are not palatable even to animals;

(ii) trunks are sold in the urban markets and the sticks are too little to meet the fuel needs of the poor in the villages, and

(iii) the farm lands are being utilised for farm forestry, resulting in a cut in food outputs. By the end of 1982-83, for instance, in Gujarat, 37 per cent of the farmers have switched from food crop farming to eucalyptus farming and even well-irrigated lands have been brought under eucalyptus farming.[24] In water scarce regions like Haryana this has the additional danger of causing a fall of the water-table in the area, whereby causing injury to lands still under foodgrains cultivation.

The net result is that food production has gone down in the relevant villages, yet the need for fuel has not been met. The shortage of food fuel and fodder continues to encourage the attack on the receding forest line to continue unabated. Thus the community interest is being relegated to the background for perpetrating self-interest.

The foregoing has to be countermanded by people's participation in planning at the grass-roots level. Commercialisation encouraged the taking of partial view of things, in all cases where positive externalities and by – products etc. were enjoyed by those who are outside the framework of markets and prices. Most important, commercialisation of agricultue resulted in commercialisation of labour. Where labour was cheap or almost free, labour intensive practices were economical up to the point where marginal product was zero, i.e., up to the point where the marginal product curve cuts the horizontal axis, where the total product curve attains the maximum, obviously taking land as the fixed input and labour the variable input. Assuming that productivity per unit of land can be increased by injecting more labour onto it, increasing labour intensity today, up to the point where the marginal product curve cuts the horizontal axis, could no longer be possible with the agriculture scene so intensely commercialised. Even small farmers find it economical to hire labour because the marginal product of labour itself was shifted up through the use of modern inputs. Even labour intensive practices which were environmentally safe, however, could not be continued in all cases were immediate marginal return to the farmer was less than the wage rate, despite the fact that the marginal return to society (or for that matter to the farmer as well) in the long—run were higher.[25]

This is the real problem. The crucial question which has to be answered here is how can resource use practices be encouraged which entails lower personal and immediate return than the cost involved, given that social and/or long term return could be higher, and discourage practices which entails lower personal costs *vis-a-vis* personal returns, given that social and or long term costs could be higher. The problem is uniform in soil erosion, free grazing, water logging and over-exploitation of natural resources.[26] The critical task of decentralised planning with the fullest and feest participation of the people in the mechanics, will seek to answer just this question.[27]

Our future lies in following the steps enshrined in the seven edicts from Jimmie Yen repeated hereunder:

"Go to the People.
Live With Them.
Serve Them.
Love Them.
Plan with Them.
Start with What They Know.
And Build on what they have".

NOTES

1. The entire gamut of the evolution of economics since at least the classical period has revolved around power-status structure. See Amitabha Mukherjee: *The Economic Theory of Resources* (New Delhi : Indus Publishing Co.) 1990.
2. This was the underlying idea of the theories of Davin, Clark and Hirschman. See A.O. Hirschman : *The Strategy of Economic Development* (New Haven : Yale University Press) 1955.
3. This is one of the Principles of Decentralised Planning. See, Amitava Mukherjee: *Foundations of Decentralisation* (New Delhi : Heritage Publishers 1990, Chapter XI and Food and Agriculture Organisation of the U.N.: *Towards Improved Multi-Level Planning for Agricultural and Rural Development in Asia and the Pacific*, FAO Economic & Social Development Paper Number 52 of 1985, reprinted in 1987, Rome.
4. The leakages one hears in the Jawahar Rojgar Yojana can not be denied but there has been no development scheme so far executed in this country where leakages were non-existent, given the overall deterioration of our social fabric.
5. A warning that Mier and Baldwin gave several decades ago, to which we have paid no attention.
6. R.P. Mishra calls this "Satellite imagery". See R.P. Misra's article in *Readings in Decentralised Planning*, Volume I edited by B.N. Yugandhar and Amitava Mukherjee, (New Delhi: Concept Publishing Co.) 1990.
7. See Amitava Mukherjee, "Decentralised Planning — A Rejoinder" in *Economic Times*, December 13th & 14th 1989, edit page.

8. O.P. Mathur in his letter to B.N. Yugandhar bearing number DIR/PS/NIUA/2963 dated 20/6/90, made a somewhat similar plausible statement: "One alternative way of looking at district planning exercise could be to begin district planning exercises in all the 410 districts at the same time without worrying about its quality. I suspect that over a period of time the quality will improve just like it happened in case of State Plans." What might be needed is to first make "it mandatory for all districts in the country and then making efforts to improve and strengthen and consolidate these exercises."
9. *See Annual Plan 1990-91*, Mysore District.
10. The criteria followed in Gujarat, Karnataka, Maharashtra and Uttar Pradesh is given in several documents. See *Report of the Working Group on District Planning* (New Delhi : Planning Commission) 1984, Vol. I.
11. Government of Gujarat: *Report on Decentralised Planning in Gujarat* (Gandhinagar, Ahmedabad : Planning Division, General Administration Department, Government of Gujarat), December 1988.
12. S.K. Ray : et . al.: *Policy Planning for Agricultural Development* (New Delhi : Tata McGraw-Hill Publishing Co. Ltd.) 1979, p. 35.
13. See K.M. Tiwari: *Address to the IV Diploma Course in Wildlife Management*, Indira Gandhi Forest Research Institute, Dehradun, as quoted in Desh Bandhu and R.K.Garg: *Social Forestry and Tribal Management* (New Delhi : Indian Environmental Society)1986.
14. Robert Wade : "Management of Common Property Resources: A Study of Some Villages in South India", *Administrator*, (Journal of the L.B.S. National Academy of Administration, Mussoorie) Vol. XXXV, No. 3, July — September, 1990, p. 60.
15. *Idem.*
16. M.L. Dewan : *People's Participation in Himalayan Eco-System* (New Delhi : Concept Publising Co.) 1989, p. 72.
17. Renu Khator : *Forest, The People and The Government* (New Delhi : National Book Organisation) 1989, p. 65. Bina Agarwal : "Rural Women, Poverty and Natural Resources", in *Economic & Political Weekly*, 28th October, 1989, is an excellent work on the issue.
18. John Robinson : *Aspects of Development and Underdevelopment*, (New Delhi : Cambridge University Press — Vikas Publishing House) 1979.
19. A.K.N. Reddy and K.K.Prasad : "Technical Alternatives and the Indian Energy Crisis", *Economic and Political Weekly*, Special Number, 1977.
20. This admittedly makes the assumption that the quality and integration of the plans framed at several tiers would improve several folds.
21. Anil Agarwal : "The Great Eucalyptus Debate", in *The State of India's Environment 1984-85* edited by S. Ninan and Anil Agarwal (New Delhi : Centre for Science & Environment) p. 65.
22. *Ibid*, pp. 63-71,
23. *Idem.* See also R.K. Kohli and Daljit Singh: "Promotion of Environmental Degradation by Eucalyptus in India", paper read at the U.G.C. sponsored 2-Day National Seminar on Environment Pollution Management in India, on 19th and 20th January 1990, at Department of Public Administration, Punjab University, Chandigarh.
24. Renu Khator : *Forest : The People & The Government* (New Delhi : National Book Organisation) 1989, p. 63. See also K.P. Singh Mahalwar: "Forest Laws and

People's Participation in Environment Protection", in R.K. Sapru and Shrama Bhardwaj: *The new Environmental Age* (New Delhi: Ashis Publishing House) 1990.

25. See M.V. Nadkarni : "Agricultural Development and Ecology-An Economists View", in H. Ramachandaran (ed.) : *Environmental Issues in Agricultural Development* (New Delhi : Concept Publishing Co.) 1989, pp. 21 to 42.
26. *Ibid.*
27. There have been in the past two methodologies propounded which sought to pay considerable attention to conservation of resources, by Professor D.R. Gadgil and Sulabh Brahme, independently of each other. Reference in invited to D.R. Gadgil: *District Development Planning*, R.R. Kale Memorial Lecture (Poona : Gokhale Institute of Economics & Politics) 1966; and to Sulabh Brahme et al. : "Regional Planning: A Case Study of Marthawada Region", *Artha Vijana* Vol. XVII, Nos. 1 & 2, 1975. None seemingly paid attention to them.

REFERENCES

Agarwal, Anil: "In the Forest of Forgetfulness", *The Illustrated Weekly of India* November 13th to 19th, 1983.

Baltiwala, S. : "Women in Poverty : The Energy, Health and Nutrition Syndrome" paper read at Conference on "Women and Poverty", at Calcutta, Centre for Studies in Social Sciences, 17th to 18th March 1983.

Bhaduri, T. and Surin, V.: "Community Forestry and Women Head-Laaders" in "Community Forestry and People's Participation", Seminar Report, Ranchi Consortium for Forestry, Nevember 20-22,1981.

Bhat, Tushar: "Ecology & Energy : Restoring the Balance", *Economic Times*, New Delhi 3/4/90.

Folger, B. and Dewan, M.: "Kumaon Hill Reclamation : End of Year Site Visit", (Delhi : OXFAM, America) 1983, mimeographed.

R.G. Lee *et. al.*: *Community and Forestry: Continuities in the Sociology of Natural Resources* (Boulder: Westview Press) 1990.

Mellor, John and Desai, Gunvant M.: *Agricultural Change and Rural Poverty* (Delhi : Oxford University Press) 1986.

Rao, C.H.H., Ray, S.K. and Subbarao, K.: *Unstable Agriculture and Drought: Implications for Policy* (New Delhi : Vikas Publishing Co.)1988.

Rao, Hanumantha C.H. : *Technological Change and Distribution of Gains in Indian Agriculture* (New Delhi Macmillan) 1975.

Nagbrahman, D. and Sambrani, Shreekant: "Women's Drudgery in Firewood Collection", *Economic & Political Weekly*, January 1st to 8th, 1978.

Swaminathan, M. : "Eight Hours a Day for Fuel Collection", *Manushi*, March — April, 1984.

Steve Tompkins: *Forestry in Crisis: The Battle for the Hills* (London: Christopher Helm) 1989.

Vaidyanathan, A.R. : *Bovine Economy in India* (New Delhi : Oxford & IBH) 198[illegible]

Zeenie's Participation in Parliamentary Elections ... Sagar, and Sogbar ... (Bhatnagar) ... (New Delhi: Ashish Publishing House, 1989).

27. There have been, in the past two-three decades, proposals which stress the ... or mutually ... to the Formation of ... Professor D.R. Gadgil ... in Kerala, independently of each other. References in this area are D.R. Gadgil, *District Development Planning*, R.R. Kale Memorial Lecture (Gokhale Institute of Economics & Politics), 1966, and ... Hadimani ..., "District Planning: A Case Study of Marathwada Region," *Artha Vijnana*, Vol. XVII, No. [illegible], 1975, which amply pay attention to them.

Bhasin, K. and Sarin, M., "Reconsidering Poverty and Women ... India," in *Community, Poverty and People's Participation*, Seminar Report, ... Corporation ..., November 20-2[illegible], 1981.

Bell, Vishal, "Ecology and Energy: Restoring the Balance," *Development Dialogue*, Nos. 1-2, 31(2), 1991.

Klar, S. and ..., "... Rajasthan ...," *Political Weekly*, Vol. XVI, No. 4, ... 1981 (manuscript).

Lee, ..., *Community and Poverty: Contributions to the Sociology of ... Formation* (London: ... Press), 1970.

Bhalla, G.S. and Alagh, Y.K., ... *Agriculture and ... Implications for Policy* (New Delhi: Vikas Publishing Co.), 1985.

Radhakrishnan, ..., "... Structural ... and ... Strategy," in ... *Economic and Political Weekly*, January 1st to 8th, 1978.

Stree Trishna, ... *The ... Justice Bill* (Madras: ... India), 1989.

Vaidyanathan, A., *Indian Economy: ...* (New Delhi: Oxford ...), 1988.

6

SUCCESSES IN DECENTRALISATION AND HOW THE FUTURE LOOKS

Nine IAS Officers*

PRELUDE

At the outset, we would like to mention that a report like the present one can be dealt with at two extreme levels. At one end, it is possible to be theoretical and give highly broad-level suggestions like revamping the existing social structure etc. and at the other, it is possible to get very detailed about the most minor nuances of district planning. We have tried to tread a path in between the two extremes because the first extreme does not appear to be very fruitful and the other extreme requires time to an extent that we never got and also presupposes adequate knowledge about the topic in advance which we never had.

We would also like to state at this juncture that we have not bothered to go into the question of defining decentralised planning, articulating the need for decentralisation etc. Such knowledge is assumed on the part of the reader.

Now, a brief account of the chapter.

Part I is divided into two parts. The first deals with the experience of such planning that the states of Karnataka, West Bengal and Gujarat have had till now. The other states have deliberately been left out due to constraints of space and also because of the fact that nothing substantial in this regard has happned anywhere else for it to merit independent comment. The second part of this chapter summarizes the

* Jointly prepared by Shri Amitabh Jain, Smt. A Shauthi Kumari, Shri Govind Mohan, Shri Manoj Joshi, Shri Pankaj Joshi, Shri Rajendra Kumar, Shri Rajiv Yadav, Smt. Subhra Rastogi and Shri Umang Narula, all I.A.S. officers (1989 Batch).

reasons as to why decentralised planning has not really succeeded till now in our country, despite the repeated attempts that have been made to give it a fillip. Also the urgency for bringing about such planning in the present milieu is elaborated.

Part II is the most important part of this report and deals with suggestions for the future as regards the steps that should be taken so as to make decentralised planning a reality. A variety of works has come out on this topic and we, by necessity have had to consult them as also to rely upon them to articulate our own recommendations. Given the constraints of time and space, it has not been possible for us to be absolutely original in our suggestions, though we have tried not to reproduce in to that which is already known. It is for the reader of this report to give the final verdict on this matter, however.

The exhibits and appendices are by way of elaborating what we have put down in the text.

I

STATUS OF DECENTRALISED PLANNING IN THE STATES

A common feature in the structure of planning machinery of the three states is the existence of two tier agencies at the district level and of a third agency at the sub-district level responsible for plan formulation. One agency at the district level is much like legislature which considers and reviews the plan put up for its approval. The other agency is responsible for formulating the schemes against the district plan outlay and for scrutinising the sub-district plans coming from the below.

The district planning body is known by different names, the Advisory body is called District Planning Board (DBP) in Gujarat, District Planning Coordination Council (DPCC) in West Bengal and Zila Parishad (Z.P.) in Karnataka. It has a varied and highly representative character. The advisory body in Gujarat and West Bengal is headed by a Minister of State while that in Karnataka by the *Adhyaksha* of Z.P. The President of Z.P. is subordinate to Collector in Gujarat but he is senior to Collector in West Bengal. Karnataka has moved a step forward by separating the regulatory and developmental functions of the district. The Z.P. is unambiguous head of the districts development and welfare administration. Collector is now responsible only for the maintenance of law and order and other regulatory functions.

In district, advisory body is assisted by an executive committee the which is known as Executive Committee (West Bengal). In Gujarat it is headed by the Collector with President of the Z.P. as its vice-chairman. In West Bengal *Sabhadhipati* is the chairman while the Collector is the Member-Secretary. In Karnataka there are nine Standing Committees (Finance and Audit, Planning and Development, Public works etc.) which are in fact executive committees. State leaders and bureaucrats find no place in these committees.

Planning have also been constituted at the sub-district level. In Gujarat and West Bengal, block (or taluka) is the unit of planning while in Karnataka it is the mandal (between block and village). Block or mandal level planning body formulate schemes against its outlay and also suggest priorities. In Karnataka there is an additional tier at the taluka level (taluka planning committee) which plays a supervisory role.

The district planning body is provided with a planning unit consisting of a chief/district planning officer, and other specialists in various fields. The chiefs/District Planning Officers work under the supervision of the Collector in Gujarat and under the *Adhyaksha* of Z.P. in Karnataka.

Distribution of Funds

Roughly 35 to 40 per cent of the State plan outlay is earmarked for the district level schemes. The district level schemes are those schemes whose benefit confines to a district only. The district-wise distribution of state outlay for these schemes is based on more or less Gadgil formula. The common indicators of the allocation formula are:

1. Total population
2. Population of weaker sections
3. Agricultural backwardness
4. Irrigational backwardness
5. Industrial backwardness
6. Communication backwardness
7. Special problems of the area and
8. Others.

Next, roughly 66 per cent to 75 per cent of the district plan outlay is earmarked to the block or Mandal with reference to formula based again on various criteria of development.

In Gujarat, the district plan outlay has three parts viz. :

(i) Outlay for normal district level schemes which constitutes nearly 80 per cent of total district outlay.
(ii) Discretionary outlays which constitute about 15 per cent of total outlay for district level schemes.
(iii) Incentive outlays to be allocated against the funds raised by the district which constitute about 5 per cent of total district outlay.

Schemes under normal district level schemes are implemented through head of departments while schemes under discretionary and incentive outlay are initiated, approved and implemented through DPB's. The DPB's finance projects on 100 per cent basis from the discretionary outlay while the incentive components of district outlay required a matching proportion of funds viz. 10 per cent, 25 per cent or 50 per cent depending upon the extent of backwardness.

In West Bengal, the funds under the direct central (united) of the planning bodies include outlay under the rural programme like JRY, IRDP, TRYSEM etc. District Plan Schemes (DPS) fund has been created to meet the critical gaps. It is an united fund and constitutes about 8 per cent of the district plan per year.

In Karnataka, the entire district plan outlay is discretionary in nature. But in reality, after providing for committed expenditures, skill over-works, ongoing schemes, matching contribution for centrally-sponsored schemes, ZP's are left with little descretion. So from 1989-90, against the head district sub-plan, an outlay of few crores is made which is available to the ZP's united fund.

The P.R. Institutions in these states also generate their own resources. But the contribution of this to the total district outlay is abysmally low.

Plan Formulation

The planning exercise in Gujarat is done under two different heads viz., Normal district level and Decentralised District (United funds) level schemes. In respect of normal district level schemes, DPB's are indicated financial ceiling against which they have to formulate their proposals. These ceilings are normally kept at a lower level than the likely size of the outlay to provide flexibility to the Head of Departments for adjustments while formulating their proposal. The DPB's collect proposal from the District Implementing Officer for sectoral schemes and from District Panchayat for Panchayat sector schemes. The executive planning committee discusses the proposal and present the final draft plan to the DPB's. DPB's approve the draft plan. Next the sectoral departments are supplied with the Draft District Plan, concerning their sectors and a copy of the District Plan is submitted to State Planning Department. The district proposals are kept in view while finalising the State Plan. Sectoral departments have been instructed to communicate the reasons of non-inclusion of any proposal contained in any district plan, to the concerned DPB's. Next the Heads of Department finalises their Annual Plan proposals with the district-wise breakup and submits it to the State Planning Department.

The planning exercise for discretionary outlay initiates at the taluka level. The TPC's formulate proposals keeping in view the need of villages within the limit of likely allocation (as communicated to it by the DPB) and also suggest priorities. The executive committee collects and scrutinises proposals for district level and taluka level schemes, and thereafter formulates scheme-wise final proposal. The DPB approves the plans. Finally, the district level implementing officers are informed about approval of schemes.

The planning process in West Bengal initiates at the village level. Each Gram Panchayat prepares a "needs statement" based on its immediate needs. Each Panchayat Samiti prepares schemes to meet the most acute problems of each Gram Panchayat, keeping in view the State's priorities. The line departments furnish the district and blockwise break up of these schemes to the District Planning Committee and Block Planning Committee, after completing the disaggregation exercise of their a plan budget. Next, the district and block level programmes and special programmes like IRDP, JRY etc. are integrated into the plan document. The district plan is then sent to the DPCC for its acceptance and approval.

A somewhat similar process is also in operation in Karnataka. MP's conduct Gram Sabhas in all the villages to formulate their own sub-plan relating to local works. MP plan becomes part of the Z.P. plan. The Z.P. is the final planning authority in the district. The Z.P. prepares the district plan, which also includes the Mandal plans, thereby giving a totally representative character to the plan. Finally, the Z.P. plan is incorporated into the State Sector plans. The State Plans are then incorporated in the state budget, which contains a link document on Z.P. outlays.

Decentralised Planning : Gujarat Style

The State of Gujarat is considered as a pioneer of DP and has an experience of about 20 years in this field. D.P. in Gujarat has taken its firm roots. The decentralisation was initiated with the introduction of a three tier Panchayati Raj Institution in 1963, when certain district level schemes were transferred to District Panchayats with allocations. In 1973, the District Planning Boards (DPB's) were set up in all districts of Gujarat. In the Fourth and Fifth Five Year Plan. DPB's were asked to formulate proposals for district level schemes with certain ceilings conveyed to them. Gujarat launched a new phase of DP from 14th November, 1980 with full autonomy at the district level. Under this new scheme approximately 20 per cent if the funds earmarked for District Schemes were placed at the discertion of DPB's and they were asked to formulate and sanction schemes against these outlays.

Distribution of Outlays

It has been decided by the State of Gujarat that at least 35 per cent of the State Plan outlays should on average be allotted for districts level schemes and 20 per cent discretionary and incentive outlays for district to enable them to take up schemes of local importance. The criteria for district-wise distribution of State outlay for district level schemes are based on a formula in which weightage are given to the factors of population, weaker sections of society and backwardness in order to achieve regional balance.

The district plan outlay has three parts viz. :

(i) outlay for normal district level schemes which constitutes nearly 80 per cent of total district outlay;
(ii) discretionary outlays which constitute about 15 per cent of total outlay for district level schemes;
(iii) incentive outlays to be allocated against the funds raised by the district which constitute about 5 per cent of total district outlay.

Schemes under normal district level schemes are implemented through Head of Departments while schemes under discretionary and incentive outlays are initiated, approved and implemented through DPB's.

From 1982-83, the DPB's have been told to set about at least 65-75 per cent from the discretionary outlay allocated to the district and distribute the same amongst taluka with reference to formula based on the following criteria of development:

(1) Population of taluka.
(2) Population of SC, ST and non SC/ST agricultural labourers.
(3) Backwardness in agriculture, irrigation, idustries, roads, drinking water, education, public health and rural electrification.

About 25 to 33 per cent of the discretionary outlay is retained at the district level for district level schemes.

The DPB's finance projects on 100 per cent basis from the discretionary outlay while the incentive components of the district outlay requires a matching proportion of funds viz. 10 per cent, 25 per cent, 50 per cent depending upon the extent of backwardness prescribed for the taluka. The distribution of the incentive outlay allocated to the district, among talukas, is done on the pattern adopted for the distribution of discretionary outlay.

Machinery for Decentralised Planning

Gujarat has adopted the Minister — Chairman model under which a Minister of State of Government (not belonging to that district) has been designated as the chairman of the DPB. DPB's have a broad-based and highly representative character. The Collector is its Vice-chairman and the President of the District Panchayat is its co-Vice Chairman. The DPB meets every 3 months and is the final authority to sanction proposals received from Taluka Committees and other institutions. DPB's prepare the Perspective Plan, Five Year Plan and annual plan of the district, frames specific schemes which have to be funded from the outlays under discretionary and incentives outlays, undertakes a regular review and evaluation of district level shcemes and removes bottlenecks, if any, in their implementation. The DPB's also submit suggestions regarding the normal district level schemes, which are incorporated to the maximum possible extent, by the sectoral departments in their annual plan proposals. The DPB is assisted by the

Executive Planning Committee chaired by the Collector with President of the District Panchayat as its Co-chairman. It has representative character built into it by the inclusion of half the number of MLA's from the district who are appointed by rotation. It meets every month and monitors the implementation of the schemes sanctioned by the DPB. It scrutinises every proposal coming up for funding from the district plan outlays. The Executive Committee also monitors the progress of the MNP in the district.

At the taluka level, taluka planning committees have been set up with SDO or DDO of District Panchayat as Chairman. It formulates proposals against the discretionary and incentive outlay of the taluka and also suggests priorities. It also reviews the progress of the work sanctioned and makes on the spot visits of sites.

Each DPB has been provided with a planning cell headed by the district planning officer who works under the direct supervision of the collector. District Planning Cell consists of two wings, namely, planning and monitoring wings.

Formulation

The planning exercise in the state of Gujarat is done under two different heads viz. Normal district level and Decentralised District (United Funds) level schemes. In respect of normal district level schemes, DPB's are indicated financial ceilings against which they have to formulate their proposals. These ceilings are normally kept at a lower level than the likely size of the outlay to provide flexibility to the Head of Departments for adjustments while formulating their proposals. The DPB's collect proposals from the District Implementing officers for sectoral schemes and from District Panchayat for Panchayat sector schemes. The Executive Planning Committee discusses the proposal and presents the final draft plan to the DPB's. DPB's approve the draft plan. Next the sectoral departments are supplied with the Draft District Plan, concerning their sectors and a copy of the District Plan is submitted to State Planning Department. The district proposals are kept in view while finalising the State Plan. Sectoral departments have been instructed to communicate the reasons of non-inclusion of any proposal contained in any District Plan, to the concerned DPB's next the Head of Departments finalise their Annual Plan proposals with the District wise breakup and submit it to the State Planning department.

The Planning exercise for discretionary outlay initiates at the taluka level. The TPC's formulate proposals keeping in view the need of villages within the limit of likely allocation (as communicated to it by the DPB) and also suggest priorities. The Executive Committee collects and scrutinises proposal. The DPB approves the plan. Finally, the district level implementing officers are informed about approval of schemes.

With a view to streamline the working of the programme for normal district plan and for discretionary outlay, fixed time schedules have been given to the DPB's by the State Planning Department.

Reasons Behind the Success

Gujarat model for D.P. has been partially successful. It has brought certain concrete as well as intangible benefits to the local people of the state. The wide experience of about two decades in D.P. has resulted in the establishment of a culture of local level planning. The practice of providing discretionary and incentive outlays at the disposal of the DPB's has tended to reduce the concentration of work at sectoral level, has generated considerable fervor at the local levels and has enabled the local level authorities to make provisions for some essential missing links which had been neglected so far. The popular enthusiasm can be visualised from the fact that during the first years (1980-82), DPB availed 91.5 per cent of the eligible incentive outlay by providing matching funds of the order of 7.64 crore. One of the appealing features of the pattern of allocation of funds by DPB is the fact that the schemes of priorities differ from district to district and also differ from that in the outlay for normal District level schemes. This shows that the DPB's have exercised their discretion to suggest schemes of local importance taking local factors into acccount. For example, during 1980-81 and 1981-82 about two-third was allocated allocated by DPB's towards schemes covered under MNP. The reasons for the success of DP in the state has been attributed to a number of factors. Firstly, the Panchayati Raj Institution has provided a firm foundation for building up and strengthening the decentralisation of the planning process. Secondly, the political leadership at the state level has played a vital role in the establishment of the institution of D.P. in the State's political structure. It has understood the advantage of D.P. and thereby has acted as a catalyst in it's implementation of it. Since the first year of the Sixth Plan, roughly 40 per cent of the State plan outlay has been earmarked for the district level schemes. A comparison could be drawn from Maharashtra where the original allocation of district level schemes had been 60 per cent of the State plan outlay but has now come down to about 25 per cent. State government of Gujarat also gives full autonomy to DPB's for scheme formulation, approval and implementation against discretionary and incentive outlays. This has aroused considerable enthusiasm among the local people. Finally, the fund allocation exercise has been carried out scrupulously from state to district and from district to taluka on rational criteria and has been accepted socially and politically.

Drawbacks

In real sense, the decentralised planning in Gujarat is confined only to 15 per cent discretionery outlay and 5 per cent incentive outlay. The planning for the 80 per cent normal district level schemes is being done at the State level only and the role of the DPB's is at best only marginal. Secondly, the planning for each of the three components in the DP exercise is carried out independently of each other with no linkages among them. An integraetd District Plan is missing in Gujarat. Moreover, the District Plans for the 15 per cent and 5 per cent sectors do not get integrated into the State Plan. It is also seen that substantial portion of the untied funds are eaten by the way of committed expenditure in form of on going schemes and non-plan expenditure.

Presently, the role of the PRI in the decentralised planning is reasonably low. The President of the District Panchayat is co-chairman both in DPB and Executive Committee of the Board. It is rightly believed that the fruits of the D.P. cannot be gained fully without giving due representation to local level bodies.

Finally, the extent of technical planning being used in Gujarat is fearfully very elementary. Planning at district level lacks scientific analysis of the problems. Since Gujarat has a strong foundation for decentralised planning, and good planning machinery at State level, a future expansion on scientific lines is not impossible.

Decentralised Planning: West Bengal Idea

Decentralised Planning in West Bengal is a new concept. It has yet to take firm roots. Historically, in 1957, the Government of West Bengal on the recommendations of the Balwant Rai Mehta Committee adopted a four-tier Panchayat structure comprising Gram Panchayats (at the village level), Anchal Panchayat (for entire groups of villages),

Anchalik Panchayat (for Blocks) and Zila Parishads (for districts). Direct elections were held for the lowest tier. But there was no political will behind such democratic decentralisation. Soon, these local bodies were superseded and no fresh elections were held for 15 years. In West Bengal the left front Government started action in 1977 on two fronts, firstly, by initiating a process of land refrom (including the operation Barga) and secondly, by politicising elections to the three-tier Panchayats in 1978 on party lines on the basis of the W.B. Panchayat Act (1973). Since then, Panchayat general elections have been regularly held (1983 and 1988) and at present there are about 3300 Gram Panhayats, 339 Panchayat Samities and 15 Zila Parishads. Next, the State Government delegated the power of implementation of programmes like IRDP, NREP, Drought Relief Programme, etc. to the Panchayat. These gave the Panchayats, experience in regards to the formulation and implementation of local level schemes. Finally, in 1985-86 the left front Government took a novel step of introducing decentralised planning in West Bengal, involving the Panchayat bodies intimately in every aspect of the planning process.

Planning Machinery

West Bengal has a three tier local level planning organisation viz. a District Planning and Coordination Council (DPCC), a District Planning Committee (DPC) and a Block Planning Committee (BPC). The BPC and DPC are both planning and executive agencies, the DPCC is like the legislative assembly which considers and reviews the plans put for its approval. DPCC has been constituted with a minister of State Government as its Chairman, President *(Sabhadipati)* of Z.P. as its Vice-Chairman and DM as its Secretary. It has a varied and highly representative character. It meets atleast twice every year and DPCC approves all district plans and programmes formulated by the DPC and reviews the progress of District level programmes from time to time. Another district level planning body called DPC has been set up with Sabhadhipati (President) of the Z.P. as Chairman and the D.M. as its member-secretary. Members of the DPC include Sabhapaties (Presidents) of all Panchayat Samities and the Tarmadhyatshas of Z.P. (the exectutive committee of the Z.P.). DPC formulates schemes within a framework of an overall plan for the district as a whole (including Department Schemes and Panchayat-run-schemes). It approves schemes up to Rs. 5 lakhs and finalises the schemes of a value more than Rs. 50 thousands formulated at the block level. DPC also reviews and moniters the implementation of District Plan schemes. The DPC meets atleast once in three months. At the block level the BPC has been set up with Sabhapati of Panchayat Samiti as Chairman and BDO as Member Secretary. The BPC prepares block level plans on the basis of needs statements prepared at Gram Panchayat level. The BPC is empowered to approve block-specific schemes with estimated costs less than Rs. 50,000. Schemes involving more than Rs. 50,000 is put before DPC for its approval. The BPC can also formulate schemes extending adjoining blocks but such schemes require the approval of the DPC. The BPC meets atleast once in two months. Both at the block and the district level, there is a standing committee for Planning and Development. It undertakes resource surveys and formulates plans for the part with which Z.P./Panchayat Samitis are concerned. The DPC and the BPC are assisted by a team of officials and experts which constitutes the Planning Cell of the district.

Methodology for Decentralised Planning

The planning process in West Bengal initiates at the village level. Each Gram Panchayat prepares a "needs statement" based on its immediate needs. Each Panchayat Samiti prepares schemes to meet the most acute problems of each Gram Panchayat, keeping in view the State's priorities. The line departments furnish the district and block-wise break up of these schemes to the DPC and BPC, after completing the disaggregation exercise of their plan budget. Next, the district and block level programmes and special programmes like IRDP NREP, etc. are integrated into the district plan document. The istrict Credit Plan is based on targets of annual plan formulated in the district. To provide proper linkages between credit requirements and availability of Institutional Finance, the representatives of the Lead Bank in the districts are invited in the meetings of DPCC. The credit plan aims to integrate the district-wise credit plans drawn up by the district planning authorities.

Implementation of department schemes is the responsibility of the concerned departments, while the implementation of Panchayat-run-schemes (e.g.-Schemes under NREP, IRDP etc.) is done through relevant Panchayat Raj Bodies. The DPC coordinates the implementation of those schemes which require joint implementation by more than one panchayati body or between a panchayati body and a department.

Sources and Devolution of Finance

Finance for the District Plan on West Bengal flow from District level component budgets of various departments, special programmes like IRDP, JRY, etc. and institutional funds. The share of the District Plans in the State plan has gone up from Rs. 156 crore in 1986-87 to Rs. 403 crore in 1988-89. Currently, share of the district plans is about 42 per cent of the state plan and the state is committed to increase it to about 50 per cent. District Plan funds have been created for execution of District plan schemes which cannot be otherwise met from flow of funds from different sources but represents the immediate needs of the people. PRI's implement the District Plan schemes under the untied "District Plan Fund" to meet critical gaps. DPF has been about 8 per cent of the district plan per year. This amount is distributed among the different districts in accordance with a formula based on population, extent of poverty and few similar criteria.

Reasons for Success

In 1978 Left Government gave a new life to the weak and defunct Panchayat of the state by politicising elections to the panchayat on party lines. Next, the land reforms were introduced through the panchayats and finally the implementation of the programmes like IRDP, IRDP, NREP, Drought Relief Programme were entrusted to the panchayats. This gave the panchayts a tremendous experience in regard to the formulation and implementation of rural development and employment programmes. Thus, the responsibility for the implementation of land reform as well as rural programmes like IRDP, NREP etc. lent vigour to the panchayat system and have been an appropriate prelude to the introduction of district planning at local levels.

Secondly, the uninterupted rule of the CPI(M) led left front since past 13 years at the state level has provided not only the political stability but also continuity in the State Government policies. A separate District Planning fund to meet critical gaps has been created by the state government. To encourage small savings, the government channellises 50 per cent of small savings collections in excess of the target to the local area through augmentation of DPF. This has encouraged small savings as well as District Planning.

The involvement of PRI in plan formulation and implementation has aroused considerable fervor and hope among the local people. The Sabhapati of Zila Parisad and Sabhapatis of Panchayats see in the proposals for DP a means of not only achieving a greater economic growth but also the long term aim of establishment of the socialistic society.

Another factor in the favour of the success of DP in WB is the fact that the CPI(M) controls most of the Zila Parisads of the state. Rarely are the Zila Parisad's superseded by the state government. ZP's are not visualised as the local level power base by the government.

Drawbacks

First though more than 40 per cent of the state plan outlay is transferred to the districts, but the funds available under the direct control of the DPC is miserably low. This includes outlays under rural programmes like NREP, RLEGP, IRDP, and DPS funds.

District plan like the centre and state plans have an overhang of an abundant amount of "Committed Expenditure". So the actual funds available at the district level to initiate new schemes based on the needs statement of the people is fearfully meagre. Also, there is a large difference between the amount under the DPS initially promised by the state government and the actually released, resulting in demoralisation of the district and block planning authorities.

Year	DPS funds promised (crores)	Actual release (crores)
1985-86	24	17.45
1986-87	30	12.38
1987-88	24	15.28

Another problem is related to the non-availability of reliable information at the block levels. Finally, the resource mobilisation by the panchayat as indicated by the following table (1987-88) is quite low.

Tier	Average of funds available (In lakhs)	Average income from own resources (In lakhs)	% resource mobilisation
Gram Panchayat	1.87	0.093	4.98
Panchayat Samities	21.20	0.21	1.00
Zila Parisad	515.00	4.00	0.78

So there is a need for improving the taxation power of the Panchayats in order to make them liable and self-reliant.

Decentralised Planning: The Miracle of the Karnataka Model

The Karnataka State as entered the third phase in the evolution of decentralised planning. In the first stage of decentralisatin (1978-82), the State Plan was bifurcated into the District Sector and State Sector Scheme. Funds were distributed between districts more or less on the basis of Gadgil formula. Next the lump sum allocation was re-allocated sector-wise by District Planning Committees. But State's Annual Plans were formulated largely independently of district plans. The schemes recommended by the district planning committees could not be Integrated into the State Plan without modification. So the District Plans underwent thorough modification at the state level. During the second phase of district planning (1982-87) a sectoral and minor headwise allocations for each district was made at the State level. All the plan schemes (including Tribal Sub-Plan, SCP), Centrally-sponsored schemes) which could be planned and implemented at the district level were brought under district sector. Provision for united funds under the head district level sub plan' was made for taking up schemes of local and immediate importance. The district planning during the first two phase revealed the inherent problems in implementing D.P. The major problem was the lack of experience of the official machinery in plan formulation and also lack of participation of local institutions in the process of District Planning. The Janata Party came to power in 1983. It introduced and passed the radical Karnataka ZP, Taluka Panchayat Samities, Mandal Panchayats and Nyaya Panchayat Bill, 1983 (discussed in the next section). Election to 887 Z.P. seats and a titanic 54,670 Mandal Panchayat seats were held in 1987. With this Karnataka entered the stage of decentralisation in which an elected district body acquired the authority to plan and implement all the development activities relevant to the districts.

The PRI Structure

The Karnataka Panchayat Bill, 1983, provides for a three-tier Panchayati Raj set up by establishing the ZP, the Taluka Panchayat Samiti, and the Mandal Panchayat (MP). The bill also brings into being the institution of Gram Sabha at village level and Nyaya Panchayat at mandal level.

Gram Sabha is the lowest tier. All those on the electoral roles of ZP pertaining to the revenue village constitute the Gram Sabha. Gram Sabha meets at least twice a year where it discusses and reviews all development programmes within the village and plans for local improvement. It also selects beneficiaries for all beneficiary-oriented programmes. Gram Sabha also discusses the report placed before it by the MP, of the development programmes relating to the village undertaken last year and those planned to be taken up during the current year.

Mandal Panchayat is the first elected tier of the system. One member for every 500 population of the mandal is elected to the MP (population of a mandal is about 10,000-11,000). Total membership ranges between 20 and 22. Total MP's are in proportion to their population. The MP elects two members as Pradhana and Up-Pradhana. Mandal Panchayat's implement all development and welfare programmes with an intra-mandal orientation. It also formulates agricultural production plan and plans for development of the panchayat area as a whole. The ZP's supervise the financial and personnel matters of MP's. The annual budget estimate of the MP requires approval from the ZP. The ZP has the power to dissolve the MP if the body "exceeds or abuses its powers" or is not competent to perform.

Taluk Panchayat Samiti at the Block level is a nominated body comprising all the Pradhans of mandals in the taluk, members of ZP and the State Legislature representing a part or whole of the taluk, and five members belonging to SC, ST, BC and women. The TPS supervises the acts of officers and servants of ZP working in the taluk, inspects work of development schemes in progress, reviews the work of MP and coordinates the inter-mandal-oriented schemes within the taluk.

The ZP is the top tier as well as second directly elected tier of the PRI. One member for every 35,000 population is elected to the ZP. There are 19 ZP's in Karnataka with about 900 directly elected members. MP's and MLA's are the nominated members of the ZP. Reservation is provided for women (25%), SC and ST. The term of office of a member is five years. The members of the ZP elect an Adhyaksha and Upadhyaksha amongst themselves. The Adhyaksha has a rank of a Minister of State and the Upadhyaksha has been equated

planning in Karnataka. First, a typical Karnataka village has a stratified rather than a polarised structure. It has three strata (elite, middle and poor) rather than two (few rich, majority of poor). It is seen that interveners for change finds it easier to reach the poor in situation of stratification than polarisation. Secondly, all the three strata have been drawn into the development process in some programme or other. The poor benefit from the wage-oriented employment generation programme while the middle state respond to the agriculture and asset programme. The elite benefit from the newer productive and remunerative opportunities in the larger economy outside the economy. Third, the coming of development programmes and funds into villages along with the revitalistion of the PRI has made the elite compete among themselves for village leadership and votes of poor by promising new local level programmes. This has loosened the traditional feudal relationship and lessened the hold of the elite on the poor.

Finally, the formulation of land army at the village level has also favoured decentralisation in Karnataka. Land Army is a corporate body consisting of able bodied men. It is organised by the state. The normal work relating to development is first entrusted to the land army. The establishment of land army has reduced unemployment as well as leakages from schemes and programmes.

Drawbacks

The new set up of decentralisation in Karnataka has been in operation for about three years. It is too early to pronounce judgement on its performance. A close study of the Karnataka model reveals some of its inherent defects.

First, theoretically the entire district plan outlay is in nature of directionary outlay. In reality after providing for committed expenditure, spillover works, MNP, on going schemes, matching contribution for centrally-sponsored schemes, ZP's are left with little freedom. So there is a need to transfer wages and salaries of the staff to the non-plan expenditure of the state. Also the matching contribution for centrally-sponsored schemes needs to be drawn from the State Plan.

Second, the quantum of resources being transferred to the Zila Parishad is not enough. The resource mobilisation at the mandal level is critically low resulting in resource-scarcity at sub-state levels.

Third, the district planning is not supplemented with district budgeting. Fourth, evidence suggests that the institution of Gram Sabha has not been successful. It does not evoke reasonable public participation and there has been almost total failure in fulfilling the prescribed functions. The lowest tier of the PRI have been burdened with responsibilities and no powers.

Finally, section 271 of the Act empowers the State Government to dissolve the ZP. Though it is an attempt to safeguard disciplinary powers at sub-state level in order to ensure effective implementation of plans and development programmes, but it does not rule out the possibility of purely political considerations playing a role.

The Reasons for Failure of District Planning to Take Roots in General Problems and Constraints

The described three models have been the success stories. Apart from these, however, there has not been much success as regards decentralised planning in the rest of the country. The reasons for these are as fallows:

Resistance-political and Bureaucratic Seen in a Reluctance to Devolve Power and Funds

Lack of proper planning machinery and data at the district level leading to mere aggregation of sectoral funds rather than planning in the true sense.

Lack of adequate finance seen in a miniscule discretionary outlay, diversion of most money to committed expenditure and lack of local revenue sources.

Lack of integration and linkages both vertical wherein district plans are not linked with the state plans and horizontal, wherein plans of different agencies operating in the districts are not linked together.

Structural reasons such as dominance of local elite and scuttling of local level leadership by the established politicians.

Imperatives of development till now like infrastructure, bank nationalisation and anti-poverty programmes which have of necessity favoured centralised decision-making.

Today, however, there is an urgent need for decentralised planning. Divisible outlays on social development and poverty alleviation programmes are becoming more important now as a percentage of plan unds. Planning for these is best done at lower levels. Secondly, people ıt the grassroots today are much more aware of their political rights han before. Universal adult suffrage and frequent and regular elections ıave ensured a greater need among people for increased participation n their own affairs.

It is in this backdrop that we must consider the next chapter.

II

SUGGESTIONS FOR THE FUTURE

Our endeavour here is to discuss six major topics which we feel to be the core of the whole argument of decentralised planning. In the discussion of these issues, we would be augmenting the views of the above committee with our own findings and opinions. These areas are:

1. Mechanisms to ensure people's participation.
2. Organisational structure at the district.
3. Data gaps and data required at the district level.
4. Finance and resources for the district.
5. Establishing linkages at the district-horizontal and vertical.
6. Project planning at district planning.

Mechanisms to Ensure People's Participation

This, in our opinion is the most important of all topics to be considered in reference to district level planning. Though this topic is very vast and would include all facets of Panchayati Raj, we would restrict our discussion only to a few broad areas. In the ultimate stages, we would suggest that planning be totally entrusted to the people under the philosophy of "people plan and government supports". Examples like the Comprehensive Area Development Programme in West Bengal and the Tilonia experiment in Rajasthan are the kind of ideals that we would wish to reach where the internal motivations of people are brought into play with the help of some external aid. The second issue is that of "who should participate?". The answer in our opinion is that the participation should be of the so-called marginalised categories — small and marginal farmers, agricultural labourers, scheduled castes and tribes, petty artisans etc. But the crucial issue is as to how to enable all such people to reach the ideal stage that we wish them to attain. This issue is dealt with in the following paragraphs.

The only way in which all this can be brought about is to let democracy come right down to the grassroots by creating viable Panchayati Raj Institutions in all districts of all states. According to us, on the basis of the study of states done by us, these institutions should have the following characteristics.

A Two-tier Structure: The uppermost level should be the district, since it has traditionally been the unit of local administration and the planning, supervision and coordination of development programmes can best be carried on from here. Also, it has the technical competence and the organised human resources to take care of all functions entrusted to it. Apart from the district, which also is far removed from the people, there should also be a tier at an intermediate level like the Mandal in Karnataka. This would be founded on a "growth" or "service" centre principle and would have all the facilities and infrastructure to enable it to render developmental activities for the entire region. More about it's constitution would be dealt with later. We wish to do away with any people's body at the lowest i.e. Gram Panchayat level. The reason is that at this level, it has been shown that there is little public participation, a total failure of all functions entrusted, lack of proper publicity of meetings, apathy of the chief, lack of finance and trained people to do any meaningful planning or even to articulate reasonable demands, poor ability to invest, create assets, use and adapt technology properly and most important, a greater chance of subversion of the genuine demands by the vested interests. We might ultimately move to the ideal of the village as "self-contained republic" but at this stage, we would recommended that there should not be much emphasis on a people's body at the village level.

Size of the Mandal: Andhra Pradesh has mandals which are co-terminus with their revenue mandals and comprise a population of about 35,000-40,000. Karnataka on the other hand, has smaller mandals with a population of 10.000-12,000. The former are in position to use the resources of the development blocks and so are technically more viable but at the same time, are also far removed from the people. Since we do not intend to have a people's body at the village level, we would suggest the Karnataka model and recommend mandals for population sizes of 10,000 or so. The kind of functions that we envisage for them as shall be brought out shortly do not need much of technical expertise at their levels.

Election: It is very essential that elections are held regularly, at fixed intervals for these bodies. This is necessary because an element of accountability must be established in the system to make the ones in power accountable to their constituencies. There must also be reservations for the maiginalised sections, i.e., the SC/STs, women, small and marginal farmers and agricultural workers and it must be ensured that these are observed in letter and spirit.

Power of Superession: We feel that the misuse that the Central government, particularly in recent times has made of Article 356 should not be replicated by the states in the case of these institutions. As such, each superior tier i.e. the State Government for the district level body and the District body for the mandal level body should be given the power to dissolve the subordinate body only on grounds of gross incompetence and/or gross abuse of the powers granted. Moreover, such powers should be appealable in the regular judicial system and judicial verdict should be made overriding over the executive direction of dissolution.

Functions Entrusted to this Body: Exhibit 2.1 gives the list of subjects that had been assigned to these bodies by the ill-fated 64th amendment of the Constitution brought out by the Rajiv Gandhi Government and an illustrative list has also been suggested in the report of the Working Group on District Planning [Annexure 5.1 Page 141 of the *Report of the Working Group on District Planning* (New Delhi: Planning Commission) 1984]. Both of them are fairly identical and contain subjects like agriculture, rural industries, animal husbandry, minor irrigation, MNP etc. Broadly, all those functions which are co-terminus with a district and which have no spill-over to adjoining areas should be assigned to the district. In devolving functions down to the mandal level, the same criterion would hold valid i.e. all the schemes which are co-terminus with mandal would be entrusted to them. However, the final decision on this division of functions should always be left to the appropriate levels, i.e. the districts and the states and no rigid guidelines should be formulated. A particular weakness that has emerged in all district planning experiences, particularly the one in Karnataka has been that most of the district funds get eaten up in the continuation of on-going schemes and maintenance of the existing set-up. This is to be avoided by the following method. First, a cut-off date is to be fixed after which district planning would be initiated. All the schemes which are on-going as on this date should be entrusted to the State Government for the purpose of completion. The district bodies should only concern themselves with those schemes which are starting anew as on this date. Secondly, all schemes at the mandal level should be designed in such a manner that they finish within one year. Given the kind of functions which these bodies would be handling, this should not be too difficult. Thirdly, not more than a specified percentage of all schemes to be taken up by the district level bodies should spill over onto the next year. Since these schemes would be inter-mandal in character and hence slightly more complex, this much leeway can be given. Finally, a perspective plan ought to be drawn up, at least at the level of the district and this should ensure that over a ten year horizon also, the quantum of spillover from one year to the next is limited.

Organisational Structure at District

At the outset, we would like to emphasise that the major problem being faced at the district level is that of horizontal and vertical coordination and the integration of the political and administrative systems present therein. The characteristics of the organisational structure that we would desire at the districts should have the following characteristics as has been recommended by the Working Group on district planning:

(a) Supremacy of people's representatives over the executive.
(b) Effective coordination and control of a single agency. This is to avoid fragmented decision-making associated with vertical hierarchies working at cross purposes.
(c) Integration under the aegis of a body of the political, district, administrative and local institutions including co-operatives and voluntary agencies.
(d) Requisite technical expertise to formulate programmes of development based upon local needs, aspirations and resources.
(e) Authority to lay down a programme of work for the implementing agencies, and of monitoring and review of the same.

In principle, we would wish to adopt the Karnataka model for the purpose of laying down the organisational structure. The reasons are that it substantially satisfies the above conditions. The executive machinery has been made responsible to the people's body both at the Mandal and the District level; all the sectoral departments at the district level have been made responsible to these bodies and the sectoral hierarchies have been removed to a large extent, leading to an integration under the aegis of the Zila Parishad of the major institutions at the district level and sufficient authority have been given to the bodies to supervise implementation of the proposed plan. It is only the extent of technical expertise that such institutions are still lacking. The essential features of the model proposed by us are as follows:

1. There should be, at the district level a body called the "Planning Cell" attached and subordinate to the district level Panchayati Raj body. The members of this body should be as per the Hanumantha Rao Committee Report, the sectoral heads of departments of all district level agencies; the lead bank representatives; the DIC representatives; the DRDA project administrator; representatives from co-operatives, the social welfare departments in-charge of SCA/TSP; all voluntary agencies and other organisations pumping money into the district and all manner of technical and professional help available at the district level.
2. We differ from the Karnataka model in one respect and that is as regards the role of the District Magistrate in the scheme of things at the district. We feel that the District Magistrate should be the chief executive of the Panchayati Raj body rather than any Chief Secretary. This model prevails in West Bengal and the biggest argument for this is the fact that law and order and development are not isolated topics and must be under the effective control of one person. If we decide to entrust law and order also to the district Panchayati Raj body, it would be all-right for a separate functionary to operate as the coordinator of the developmental planning and implementation works. But since such a step might not be contemplated so early, as the panchayati Raj bodies would still be very nascent, the district magistrate must also function as the chief executive officer of the district panchayat and the head of the planning team. It is said that an overworked officer might not be able to give enough time to this aspect. To answer this argument, we would suggest that the report of the Working Group on District Planning be followed and an officer called the Additional District Magistrate appointed in all states (he is there at many places already) to relieve the District Magistrate of routine

work. Furthermore, security of tenure for a period of at least 3 years must also be provided to the District Magistrate to ensure some continuity in day to day functioning. Serious steps ought to be taken in this direction.

3. Another step that needs to be taken is that of developing a cadre in each state of a service of planners who would be drawn from disciplines like economics, statistics, agriculture etc. and the post of a District Planning Officer ought to be created in each district to take care of the nitty-gritties of planning. Till such time that a service like this is created, we must rely on extensive training of officers from other departments as also help from the state level planning authorities to develop simple district plans. The District Planning Officer should be the member-secretary of the planning cell. This is a recommendation of the working group but has not been followed in spirit anywhere.

The Mandal Level Structure

4. The structure at the mandal level would be as follows: At the level of each block, there should be a body analogous to the Taluka Samiti in Karnataka. This would comprise of all the chairmen of the various mandal level bodies falling under the block and the local MLAs. The office of the Block Development Officer would be an office attached and subordinate to this body and would largely be responsible for the carrying out of the various plans decided upon. It should also have the necessary technical capabilities to do the kind of planning that it would be required to. In our set-up the office of the Sub-Divisional Officer is a purely law and order-cum-revenue body and we have not envisaged any role for him in the developmental side.

5. The issue of how to make the various executive heads subordinate to the people's body is very important. It is suggested that the basic power of making financial allocations would rest with these bodies and that would be a major source of control. Secondly, there should be a column related to the performance in district planning and implementation in the confidential rolls of all the officers. Although this column would finally be filled by their appropriate seniors, but it would be done on the recommendations of the chairman of the

appropriate level body. For the Block Development Officer and other block level functionaries, this would be done by the members of the Taluka level body, and for the District Magistrate and other sectoral district chiefs, this would be done by the chairman of the district level body. The power of appeal against a senior officer who refuses to pay heed to such recommendations would lie with the state government. The power of implementation of the plans would be with the various sectoral departments but the monitoring would be done by standing committees which would have as it's members the relevant sectoral chiefs, the District Magistrate, Block Development Officer and the chairman etc. of the appropriate government department. The staff of the Group "C" and Group "D" could, however, be incorporated within the district and mandal level bodies on a permanent basis.

6. The final recommendation as regards the organisational structure at the district level pertains to the rationalisation of district sizes on some scientific criteria, mainly, population so as to bring about some uniformity in administration and to remove the preferential bias which small districts get over bigger ones.

Finances at the District Level

One of the biggest problems existing at the district level in regards to planning is the inflow of money from a lot of diverse sources like the DRDA, SCA/SCP, TSP, DIC etc. This is something which creates many problems of integration since all these schemes have different guidelines and co-ordination of all these guidelines proves to be a stupendons task. Furthermore, it has been found that a major portion of this money lapses or is siphoned off with the result that the benefit to the poor is very little. Since we have decided to trust the people to do their own development, it would be better to remove all such lending and instead, devolve the sum total of all the money that would have come under the various schemes at one go to the district level body, viz., Zila Parishad.

The above recommendation is as regards the central funds. As regards the funds, being devolved from the state, the percentage of such devolution to be earmarked for the district cannot be fixed as a single figure for all districts. This is because the commitments of states on schemes like major irrigation, state transport, power etc. which are of necessity, inter-district in character varies from state to state. Also, the allocation percentage should not be a static figure, but one which is likely to change from one year to the next and hence subject to reviews. On account of these reasons, a body like the Panchayati Raj Finance Commission of Karnataka should be constituted in each state to determine, on a dynamic basis, the principle of devolution. The Working Group on District Planning has recommended that the percentage of allocation should be arrived at after considering the residual amount left after the state sector schemes are met on the one hand and the residual amount left after providing for all district level schemes on the other. The two figures could now, be reconciled. We agree with this recommendation and feel that it takes care of the objections raised earlier as regards fixing a static and uniform percentage of devolution for all states. Similarly, the amount to be devolved to the mandals must also be determined in a likewise manners.

The inter-se allocation among districts on the one hand and among the mandals on the other must be fixed on the basis of a modified Gadgil formula which takes into account the population, area and level of development of a district. This formula, as is the case of a few states is shown in the *Report of the Working Group on District Planning op cit.* 1984. The amount of money must be totally untied and totally at the discretion of the district level body. Furthermore, the expenditure ongoing schemes must be minimised as per the earlier recommendations.

The example of a "matching" grant, whereby people are given an incentive for raising their own resources (as followed in Gujarat) is quite unique and must be followed elsewhere. It generates self-reliance and popular participation. The taxation powers relating to land revenue, cess (or, *chowkidari*) tax, octroi, road tax, tax on interest earned by banks from rural areas and the power of retaining the small savings that are generated in rural areas must be left to the districts for the purpose of revenue raising. The matching contribution percentage should be on a one to one basis in all districts except the backward ones where it can be higher (say, three to one).

Linkages at the District Level

Before we come to the issue of linkages, it would be appropriate to dwell on the kind of planning that we have envisaged. The planning at the district and mandal levels should be a blend of people's participation and technical expertise and each should be tempered by the other so as to generate a "political operational culture". Now we turn to the issue of vertical linkages. Once the amount of funds being sent from the centre to the district, the principles of devolution from the state to the districts and and from the districts to the mandals are decided upon, the mandals would be in a position to know well in advance as to the approximate amount of funds that they are likely to get in the coming financial year. The states and the districts are advised to err on the side of caution herein indicating the percentage step up in the total funds being devolved downwards so as to keep a cushion for any "resource crunches" from the next higher level. Once the mandals know this figure, they can start the process of planning involving consultations among the members of the body as also with the residents of the area concerned in order to generate a list of their problems and that of suggested schemes to obviate these. This process should start in the lean season, say the second week of February of the year preceding the one for which planning is being done in order to ensure that the farmers are free to participate and not working on their fields. These schemes can be handed over to the BDO by the end of the second week of March. The BDO can now use the techniques of project planning, outlined in the next section to generate a list of his own schemes which he feels is suitable to the area. This process must end by the last week of March. In the first week of April, the entire Taluka level body can meet and the two sets of schemes can then be reconciled to arrive at a final list by the first week of May. This consolidated list can be now given to the district level body. On the basis of this list, the problems of the district as perceived by the district planning cell on an analysis of the data pertaining to the district and the opinions of the people, a list of schemes which are inter-mandal in character and hence, within the purview of the district level body can be formulated. The rough draft of this plan must be ready by the first week of July. Now a full meeting of this body can be convened (so as to avoid assembly sessions) and final decision can be taken on the schemes to be taken up at this district level as well as on the final allocation to be made to the mandals on the basis of the final funds picture that will emerge now. (Some mandal level may have to be toned down, but, by and large the district level bodies should not have any substantial powers of altering the plans that have been prepared at the mandal level.) This plan must be ready by the last week of

September to be voted in the legislative assembly in it's winter session i.e. November.

The second problem of integration is horizontal i.e. integration of the district plan with the district credit plan. Some people argue that the two cannot be integrated as the former deals with community benefit schemes while the latter deals with individual beneficiaries. This argument is not acceptable since all individual schemes e.g. loan for a milch cow has to be done in tendon with appropriate community schemes e.g. construction of milk road so as to ensure the cow's viability. To enable a dovetailing of one with the others the meeting of the DLCC must start in the month of May when all mandal level plans have been received and while the process of preparation of district plan is underway. These meetings must be interactive and the help and advice of the BDO's must be sought regularly. On the basis of these meeting a rough Annual Action Plan (AAP) must be ready by end september when the district plan has acquired a final shape. Since the AAP need not be voted in legislature, it can be refined further, so that by December it has acquired a final shape. The answer to the problem of horizontal and vertical integration is efficient time-tabling and if the above procedure is followed, there should not be any problems in this regard.

Data Management

The first thing to be borne in mind here are the current sources of data. These are as follows:

(a) The census data, which furnishes population related figures decadally.
(b) The quinquennial live-stock census which provides information on the size and composition of livestock.
(c) The NSS data on income, expenditure and level of living of people including the extent of poverty and unemployment. These, data, however, is aggregated only at the state level but the state figures can be brought down to District level data by the application of an appropriate allocator.
(d) The "village Index Card" scheme, started in 1986 which collects data on 27 developmental indicators at the village level and has been started in some states like Karnataka, Gujarat and Madhya Pradesh.

(e) Data collected by various line departments during implementation of various programmes. Thus, the agricultural department has data on land use and cropping pattern, health department has it on the medical facilities available in the district, etc. These data, however, remains with these departments only and rarely flows up to the body e.g. the Directorate of Economics and Statistics, which is supposed to compile it.

Inadequacies in the Existing System:

(a) Inadequacy or non-availability of data leading to a huge data gap. The committee of the study Group on Information Gap, constituted by the Planning Commission has highlighted the following major areas of deficit data:

(i) Utilisation/classification of land, cropwise area, typewise irrigated area, land holdings etc.
(ii) Data on forests including the digraded areas.
(iii) Sources and potential of irrigation in the districts.
(iv) Information on small, marginal, SC and ST Farmers including their proportion below poverty line.
(v) Unemployment/underemployment positions of different categories.
(vi) Income and consumption levels in the district.
(vii) Inflows and outflaws of goods and services from and to the district.
(viii) Data on income estimates for the district.

Some Suggested Measures

(a) Taking into account the above data gaps, the committee mentioned above has listed on extensive set of data that needs to be collected at the village, block and district levels. It has also stated the proposed mechanism whereby this could be done. In addition, the following points have been mentioned.
(b) The 38th and 43rd rounds of NSS published data on income and unemployment aggregated at the state and National levels. In the successive rounds, it must increase the level of deseggregation to cover at least the districts (as has been done

in respect of Andhara Pradesh). If not the blocks and villages. The sampling techniques might be adequately modified, for this purpose.

(c) The work done by the Wadia Institute of Himalayan Geology, Dehradun has been remarkable in collecting data for Pauri district of U.P., under the scheme of Natural Resources Data Management System (NRDMS). Besides this, the data collected by NISTADS, Delhi for Gurgaon; by CSRE, IIT, Bombay for Kheda, ORG, Bhubnesware for Korapat; AMU, Aligarh for Sultanpur and INCOR, Andhra University for Visakhapatnam; all under the auspices of the same scheme has also been quite comprehensive. NRDMS has emerged as a major success in the field of data collection and we strongly recommend that it be, introduced in the other districts also. The efforts of this system can be used in conjunction with the facilities of DISNIC to make all the data on-line in identical formats. (Refer Exhibit 2.4 for a schematic diagrams showing the operation of NRDMS).

(d) Lastly, there has to be an effective machinery for the validation of the collected data and the State Directorate of Economics and Statistics can think in terms of carrying out sample checks of the data maintained at the district in order to lend reliability to it.

Project Planning and Methodology

A Mandal Level Body (MLB) would cover normally ten villages, therefore, it would have a population of about fifteen thousands. These bodies should look for causative problems rather than symptomatic problems. For example, both low income and malnutrition are problems, but low income is a causative problem and malnutrition is a symptomatic problem.

Then, Mandal Level Bodies should chalk out the schemes which could solve the problems of their area. One scheme might solve even more than one problem and similarly more than one scheme might be needed to solve a single problem. Again, all the schemes should be arranged in order of preference by the MLBs. While preparing the scheme, the MLBs should keep in mind the amount of money, that they are likely to get from District Plan (which must have been indicated to them by district authorities). At the same time, at the block level, the Block Development Officer should prepare Mandal Plans for all the

Mandals which comes under that block.

The plan prepared for the mandals by the Block Development Officer should have a scientific and mathematical backing. Scalogram and Schemogram should be prepared for this purpose. One of the simple methodology, which could be applied for the preparation of plans, has been explained in Appendix I. The schemes prepared under the plan would normally not exceed the anticipated funding. The block officers should also give sufficient weightage to the points, which have been recommended by the working group on district planning.

Next, the block level officers and the MLB would meet with their respective plans for that Mandal. All those schemes, which are high on the priority list of both groups, should be accepted immediately. There may be a scheme, which is high on the priority list of block officers but low on the priority list of the MLBs. For such schemes, the block officers should convince the MLBs about the suitability of the scheme. Normally, they should be able to convince the MLBs, because the schemes prepared by them have solid mathematical backing and they have been formulated on the basis of actual data collected. But, in case the MLB is insistent on another scheme, that scheme should be accepted, that is, by and large all schemes selected should be on the basis of consensus for enlisting better local level peoples' participation.

All the Mandal Plans should be prepared in the same way, and should be sent to the District Body, so that the overall district plan becomes an integrated plan.

At the district level, the District Level Body (DLB) should approve the plan prepared by MLBs keeping in view the funds that they are likely to get. Some adjustments in the amount of fund to be given to a particular MLB can always be made depending on the requirements of that MLB.

The District Level Plans

The analysis of the data collected about the district would give a profile of the district and therefore would suggest a definite long term strategy for it's development. The district plan should have only those schemes which would be in accordance with the long term strategy as brought out by the database. For example, the profile of the district may be of dependence of dry land forming, of one of extensive irrigation potentialities, or one of major urban hinterland. The district plan for the first district should concentrate mostly on conservation of soil and water, afforestation and other such investments, second district should concentrate on development of that potential, which may be in the form of a programme of construction of wells or water conveyance under a major irrigation project. Similarly, the third district should concentrate on skill formation and provision of workshop facilities, which would be in consonance with it's profile of major urban hinterland.

Keeping the broad-level objectives as outlined above in mind, the task of preparing district level plans can start. The first priority should be given to the schemes linking two or more schemes of different MLBs. For example, in a district there may be two nearby blocks which are connected to the district headquarters by good roads, but there is no road connecting these two blocks. In this case, District Sector Plan may provide for a road connecting these two blocks. If further funds are available out of the amount retained at the district level, then projects and schemes thought in accordance with the long term plan should be taken up.

Mandal Level Bodies should also have the Knowledge of long term plan of the District, so that they don't recommend the schemes which the DLB is going to take up in near future, say in next three years, as a part of it's long term plan. Instead they can opt for other schemes and can make better utilisation of their funds.

REFERENCES

Books

Dubey, K.N.: *Planning and Development in India*; Ashish Publishing House; 1990.

Rao, C.H. Hanumantha: *Report of the Working Group on District Planning Parts I & II*; Planning Commission; Government of India;1984.

F.A.O. Report: *Towards Improved Multilevel Planning for Agricultural and Rural Development in Asia and Pacific*; 1985.

Kumar, T.M. Vinod & Mahavir: *District Planning: A state of the Art Survey*; Department of Urban and Regional Planning, School of Planning and Architecture, 1990.

Mukherjee, Amitabha: *District Planning in West Bengal—A report on Malda District*; 1989. (Manuscript available with the District Planning Unit Lal Bahadur Shastri National Academy of Administration, Mussoorie).

Planning Commission: *Report of the Committee of the Study Group on Information Gap*, 1989.

District Planning Committee, Midnapore *Village based District Planning Process — An Outline of Methodology*: 1986. Manuscript available with the District Planning Unit, Lal Bahadur Shastri National Academy of Administration, Mussoorie.

ARTICLES

Ghosh, Arun: "Decentralised Planning: West Bengal Experience"; *Economic and Political Weekly*, March 25th, 1988.

Nair, Janaki; "Karnataka : Zila Parishad Elections"; *Economic and Political Weekly*; January 24th, 1987.

Rao, V.M. :"Decentralised Planning: Priority Economic Issues"; *Economic and Political Weekly*; June 24th, 1989.

Rao, C.H.Hanumantha ;"Decentralised Planning: An overview of experience and Prospects in India".

APPENDIX I

Part A

(1) Schemes having high employment potential should be given high priority. It is better to devise programmes, which would give employment to the people in their existing occupations.
(2) Quick results with minimum investment can be obtained, if all under-utilised resources are more fully exploited.
(3) Complementary and Supplementary investments are likely to maximise the yield potential of past investments.
(4) Many times potential resource remains neglected, because they are considered to be unproductive, a suitable example is scrub jungle under the forest department.
(5) Schemes which can utilise the locally available labour should be preferred.
(6) New schemes, which are proposed, should be coordinated with ongoing and completed ones.
(7) Every scheme should have schemes with it, which would provide forward and backward linkages to it, so that the programme does not fail.

Part B

To start with, it is essential to have complete information of the nature and number of functions present in each settlement in the study area. Once these data are collected and processed it is possible to assign weights (relative importance) to each level of a function:

Functions	No. of Settle-ments Having the Function	No. of Settlements	Weight
(1)	(2)	(3)	(4)
High School	10	500	50
Junior High School	50	500	10
Primary School	250	500	2

(Contd.)

(1)	(2)	(3)	(4)
Branch Postoffice	100	500	5
Dispensary	50	500	10
Bank	25	500	20
Cycle Shop	100	500	5

The settlement could be anything, depending on what one is planning for. For District Planning the settlement could be villages. The weight of a function is given by:

$$\text{Weight} = \frac{\text{No. of settlements in the District}}{\text{No. of settlements in the district having the function}}$$

Based on the hierarchy of functions, an hierarchy of settlements in the study area can be identified using the following procedure:

First a matrix should be prepared in which all settlements are arranged in the first column in ascending order of population and the weights of all functions located in each settlement are shown individually in rows in order of population size and the weight of all functions opposite the settlements (one such example is shown in table 1A).

TABLE 1A: Population Size and the Weight of All Functions

Population (in '000)	Seed Distribution Centre	High School	Bank	Primary School
8.00	2	2	2	4
7.00	1	3	1	4
6.50	1	1	1	3
6.00		1	1	3
5.30		4	2	3
5.00		3	1	2
4.20		1	1	2
4.00		1	1	2
3.90		1	1	2
3.60			1	1
3.10			1	1
2.90			1	1
2.00				1
	6.5	3.9	3.1	2.9

From such a matrix it will be observed that some functions are found in all settlements, while some are found only in a few. The population size at which a function appears for the first time in the matrix is known as the threshold. In all the planning exercises the settlements who are below the threshold level should be given the first priority.

EXHIBIT 1.1

GUJARAT

DISTRICT PLANNING BOARD

|

MINISTER OF STATE (Chairman)

|

DISTRICT COLLECTOR (Vice-Chairman)

|

PRESIDENT OF THE DISTRICT PANCHAYAT (Co-Vice-Chairman)

|

DISTRICT PLANNING OFFICER (Member-Secretary)

|

MEMBERS

1. Taluka Panchayat Presidents of 2 or 3 Panchayats
2. MP's, MLA's
3. President of one of the Municipalities
4. Mayor of the Municipal Corporation
5. Municipal Commissioner
6. Representative of District Lead Bank
7. Chairman of District Credit Cooperative Bank
8. District Development Officer
9. Member State Planning Board:

D.P.B. approves the draft plan prepared by the Executive Planning Committee. EPC scruitnises proposals coming up for the funding from the district plan outlays including proposals from EPC.

EXECUTIVE PLANNING COMMITTEE

|

DISTRICT COLLECTOR (Chairman)

|

DISTRICT PANCHAYAT PRESIDENT (Co-Chairman)

|

DISTRICT PLANNING OFFICER (Member Secretary)

|

DISTRICT STATISTICAL OFFICER (Additional Member Secretary)

|

3 MLA's OF DISTRICT | DDO | PROJECT ADMINISTRATOR TRIBAL AREA PLAN

Tribal Planning Committee formulates proposals looking at the needs of villages and also suggest priorities against the discretionary and incentive outlay of taluka.

TALUKA PLANNING COMMITTEE

SDO/DDO (Chairman)

TALUKA PANCHAYAT PRESIDENT	MAMLATDAR	ELECTED MEMBERS OF TALUKA	CHAIRMAN SOCIAL JUSTICE COMM.	TDO (Member Secretary)

EXHIBIT 1.2

WEST BENGAL

D.P.C.C.

MINISTER OF DISTRICT (CHAIRMAN)

DISTRICT MAGISTRATE (MEMBER-SECY)	SABHADHIPATI OF UZP (VICE-CHAIRMAN)	ALL MLA's & MP's (MEMBERS)	ALL DISTRICT LEVEL OFFICERS (MEMBERS)

DPCC APPROVES THE PLAN PREPARED BY DPC

D.P.C.

DISTRICT MAGISTRATE (MEMBER-SECY)	SABHADHIPATI ZP(CHAIRMAN) SAMITIES(MEMBER)	ALL SABHADHIPATI OF PANCHAYAT	ALL DLO'S (MEMBERS)

B.P.C.

BDO (MEMBER)	SABHAPATI OF THE P.S. (CHAIRMAN)	BLOCK LEVEL AND SUBORDINATE LEVEL OFFICERS(MEMBERS)

EXHIBIT 1.3

KARNATAKA

(i)

ZILA PARISHAD

PRESIDENT OF ZILA PARISHAD

ELECTED MEMBERS (ONE MEMBER FOR THOUSAND POPULATION) RESERVATION FOR WOMEN SC AND ST ETC.	ASSOCIATED MEMBERS (CHAIRMAN OF DISTT. CENTRAL CO-OPERATIVE BANK)	NOMINATED MEMBERS(MP'S, MLA'S, MLC'S)

(ii)

TALUK PANCHAYAT SAMITI

M.L.A.(CHAIRMAN)
B.D.O.(SECY)

MEMBER OF ZP	MLA's, MLC's	PRADHANS OF MANDAL PANCHAYATS	PRESIDENT OF PLDB & TAPCMS	CO-OPTED MEMBERS

(iii)

MANDAL PANCHAYAT

PRADHAN (CHAIRMAN)
UPA-PRADHAN
(VICE CHAIRMAN)
One member for every 500 population
Reservation for women, SC, ST etc.

(iv)

GRAM SABHA
All those on the electoral rolls of Zila Parishad pertaining of the revenue villages.

EXHIBIT 2.1

(LIST OF SUBJECTS TO BE GIVEN TO PR BODIES)

1. Agriculture, including agricultural extension.
2. Land improvement and soil conservation.
3. Minor irrigation, water management, and watershed development.
4. Animal husbandry, dairy and poultry.
5. Fisheries.
6. Social and farm forestry.
7. Minor forest produce.
8. Small scale industries, including food-processing industries.
9. Khadi, village and cottage industries.
10. Rural housing.
11. Drinking water.
12. Fuel and fodder.
13. Roads, culverts, bridges, ferries, waterways and others means of communications.
14. Rural electrification, including distribution of electricity.
15. Non-conventional energy sources.
16. Poverty-alleviation programmes.
17. Education, including primary and secondary schools.
18. Technical training and vocational education.
19. Adult and non-formal education.
20. Libraries.
21. Cultural Activities.
22. Markets and fairs.
23. Health and sanitation, including hospitals, primary health centres and dispensaries.
24. Family welfare.
25. Women and child development.
26. Social welfare, including welfare of the handicapped and mentally retarded.
27. Welfare of the weaker castes and in particular of the SC/STs.
28. Public distribution system.
29. Maintenance of community assets.

Source: Article 243B of the Unsuccessful 64th Amendment to the Constitution, 1989.

7

EXTENSION OF AGRO-CLIMATIC REGIONAL PLANNING TO DISTRICT LEVEL AND BELOW:

Some Thoughts for Consideration

D.N. Basu and S.P. Kashyap

Background

The Agro-climatic Regional Planning (ACRP) project of the Planning Commission initiated in mid-1988 has completed successfully its first phase. This exercise which marked its departure from the previous macro or sectoral planning approach has focused on an integrated and holistic approach to agricultural development within the framework of resource constraints and potential of each region and thereby developing a strategy for enhancing agricultural production through optimum utilisation of land and water resources in a sustainable framework.

The distinctive merit of the ACRP approach was evident while evolving strategy and programmes at *sub-regional* level consisting of a group of districts and having a greater degree of commonalty of the relevant basic features of Soils, Topography, Climate and Water Resources than that at the 15 Agro-climatic Zonal level.

The natural corollary of the experience gained so far at ACRP will be to extend it in such a manner as to satisfy two objectives:

(a) Integrate this planning approach with decentralised planning and decision-making framework so as to make it more *realistic and people-oriented.*

(b) Integrate the planning process with implementation mechanism by taking into account what can be considered *ground realities in terms of administrative and institutional set up as well as appropriateness and replicability of technical solutions* in a given socio-economic context.

In this context, district level exercise should be considered as an *extension of ACRP approach* and not to be interpreted as preparation of *district plan per se*. As district is both an administrative unit and lowest unit considered for the purpose of formation of Agro-climatic sub-region, this process will facilitate *implementation* of strategies and programmes.

As this approach will be rather innovative and at the same time has to maintain its link with the work done as a part of ACRP, it is considered desirable to carry out this exercise at this stage on a *pilot basis during the current year*. If found relevant and practical, this can be institutionalised and made an *integral part of the comprehensive decentralised planning approach for the IX Plan.*

Approach

Given the overall context, as described above, in which the extension of ACRP is being conceived, the essential features of the suggested approach in carrying out this task are briefly described below:

(a) While the *starting point* of the exercise would be the strategies and thrust programmes as suggested in the sub-zonal/zonal level plan (in which a particular district is located), it is important to underscore that this suggested strategies and programmes need not be considered sacrosanct and can get modified on the basis of ground realities. In this sense, the plan at district level will on the one hand bear an organic relationship with the sub-zonal/zonal strategies and on the other hand be modified or made more specific to suit to *spatially disaggregated unit below the district level*. Such disaggregation can be done either on Agro-climatic Consideration or on the basis of administrative/ institutional factors.

(b) An extension of the above approach might suggest that the decentralised planning process should be *iterative rather than hierarchical*. This is based on the premise that certain planning ideas or proposals (e.g. drainage plan on watershed or river basin concept, crop production technology which crosses the space barriers) may be highly relevant in a given space context which the planners at lower hierarchical level may fail to comprehend and conversely certain planning proposals *conceptually relevant* at higher level might (e.g. Wasteland development on private and common property land, restoration of Tank irrigation) appear inappropriate or *difficult to implement* in the context of local institutional set-up or prevailing land tenure system. *Recognition of such ground realities and iterative process is perhaps the only effective way of making decentralised planning* (as applied to agriculture and allied sectors) *a meaningful one.*

(c) A clear identification and recognition of ground realities, in so far as they influence the relevance and effectiveness of any strategy or programme, will be one of the important initial steps in carrying out this district level exercise. It is difficult to list out all the dimensions which should be considered in this respect and they might also vary from one situation to another. However, as a general guideline, the following are listed:

(i) *Grass-root Level Institutions:* elected bodies, government departments or agencies, voluntary organisations, any other community-based organisations.
(ii) *Land Tenure System* and its administration.
(iii) Availability of *public goods* — common property resources, physical and social infrastructure facilities, research outfits.
(iv) Prevailing community structure and established *perceptions and preferences* in relation to development priorities and programmes.
(v) *Technology adoption or diffusion process as observed in relation to programmes* of relevance to ACRP exercise. Cost effectiveness of alternative technologies in the context of *local conditions.*
(vi) *Management* of relevant development projects and nature and extent of *peoples' participation* in the same.
(vii) An appraisal of existing *delivery system* pertaining to agriculture and allied sector.

(d) While it is recognised that the thrust of the enquiry in the district study will be on Land and Water Resources

Development Programmes, Cropping Pattern rationalisation as well as some of the Employment and Income generation activities like Livestock and Dairy, Agro Processing, it will be necessary to have a brief assessment of the *linkages of the thrust area programmes with the rest of the sectors.*

Common Objectives

While the background and approach presented above will give fairly good idea of the content and output of the district level ACRP exercise, it would not be appropriate to restrict the scope of the exercise if *additional dimensions* are considered relevant in understanding and evolving the strategies for a particular district or its sub-divisions. Similarly, some of the complexities, including institutional or agro-climatic variations *within a district* or bearing of local conditions on the cost effectiveness of a given technology, may not be relevant in case of some districts. With this consideration, an attempt has been made to describe what can be called, the *minimum common objectives* of the district level ACRP exercise.

(a) Divide the district *wherever appropriate* into further Agro-climatic or Administrative Units for each of which a brief Profile, Strategy and Indicative Plan should be prepared.

(b) Using a ZPT/ARPU document as a base for Zonal/Sub-Zonal strategies and programmes works out *detailed scheme of prioritisation and strategies and programmes* at district and sub-divisional level. *Logic of prioritisation* should take explicitly into account the natural resource endowment and their level of utilisation, peoples needs and priorities, availability of institutional and physical infrastructure, and *cost effectiveness and replicability of suggested technologies*. Programmes included in the district study could be limited, but should form the *core* of agriculture and allied sectors development.

(c) Assess existing institutional framework, in the sense in which it has been used in the section on approach and suggest both *short term and long term institutional frameworks which will facilitate implementation of priority programmes on a self sustaining basis.* In particular, recommendations should include the *specific role* of financial institutions, government agencies, research institutions, land administration, voluntary agencies and more importantly local elected bodies including Gram Panchayat and Zilla Parishad.

(d) Based on recommendations under (b) and (c) above, work out an *indicative plan for next 10 years for the district as a whole* including physical targets and financial implications.

(e) Prepare a *preliminary* employment and land budgeting based on the above indicative plan with particular reference to rural population. This aspect of work can be limited in scope in view of incomplete treatment of sectors other than agriculture and allied sector. However, it is expected that certain parallel studies will be initiated on pilot basis to bridge this information and complete the planning exercise at district level.

Database

It is recognised that in an innovative exercise of this type, database has to be flexible and will vary according to local requirements. However, two aspects need to be kept in view namely:

(a) Unlike usual statistical surveys, reliance has to be placed more on in-depth interviews and observations at lowest level i.e. village level organisation, beneficiaries and an individual project/programme management.

(b) There should be a *common database* so that *inter-district comparisons* are possible.

With regard to the common database, the following are suggested:

(i) District and sub-divisional profile in terms of Land and Water Resources Inventory, changes in Land Use Pattern, Agricultural Performance, Allied Sector, Support System almost *in line with sub-regional profile* carried out in the first phase exercise.

(ii) Inventory of project and programmes in the priority sectors at district and sub-divisional level.

(iii) An in-depth assessment of existing land tenure and administration.

(iv) Summary results of evaluation studies on *various programmes* including *technology diffusion process* carried out by government agency, independent organisation or as a part of the present exercise.

(v) In-depth discussions and interviews with block/village level organisations, community representatives, *individual beneficiaries* in farm and non-farm sector, representatives of *voluntary organisations*. Information generated from such discussions should, on the one hand, provide the basis of judging *peoples' perceptions and priorities* and on the other hand describe the *process of administration* by implementing agency and adoption of selected programmes by the beneficiary (community or individuals).

(vi) An in-depth enquiry into crop and non-crop *research efforts and their transfer* to farming community.

(vii) An assessment of the *role* of various public sector agencies including State and Central Government Departments, Banks and Cooperatives.

8

DATA-BASE FOR DECENTRALISED PLANNING*

Padma Ramachandran

This paper attempts to review, in terms of availability and limitations, the present data-base for decentralised planning in one State — Kerala, with a view to identify data gaps and suggest improvements. Except for some difference of details, the position is likely to be same in the most states.

The present data-base has been built up to meet the requirements of macro-level planning. Time series data on important variables at state level, with district level break up in some cases, are available and are being updated regularly.

Decentralised planning at district level was introduced in Kerala by the end of the Sixth Plan, in a limited way, for the implementation of schemes for the development of scheduled castes and scheduled tribes. This allocation, known as the Special Component Plan (SCP) for Scheduled. Castes and Tribal Sub Plan (TSP) for Scheduled Tribes, has been for about 10 per cent of the total plan outlay. During the current financial year, allocation for decentralised planning has been substantially increased to about 30 per cent of the total plan outlay, covering more sectors. With the implementation of the proposed decentralised administration at district level and further decentralisation of planning under way the need for building a database for decentralised planning and administration has assumed added importance. The preparation of credit plan by financial institutions also requires data at panchayat and block levels. But there is a wide gap in the availability of reliable data in time for decentralised decision making. Due to the absence of micro-level data, just decisions could not be defended nor unjust decisions challenged.

District Data Bank

The State Department of Economics and Statistics is the nodal agency for collection, processing and publication of statistics in Kerala. Basic population details at District, block and panchayat levels are available from the census publications like (1) Population Totals (Vol. III), SC and ST. Vol. IV; Workers and Non-Workers Vol. V. These are published within three years after the census. But the detailed data at lower level units are published in District Census Hand Books which become available to the data users after a long period. For example, the District Hand Books of 1981 Census relating to majority of Districts in Kerala have not yet been printed by the Government Press.

To minimise the time lag between collection and publication of data, processing of the data has to be done at district level, utilising the computer facilities available with the District Informatics Centre under the Planning Commission. A district data bank can be built up using this computer facility, there by achieving a significant improvement in the information system for decentralised planning as part of a national net work.

Lack of Coordination

There is lack of coordination among different agencies in the collection of data. For example, the meteorological data are collected by the Central Government through the Director General of Meteorology, by the state government through Revenue Department, Public Works (Irrigation) Department, Kerala State Electricity Board and Centre for Water Resources Management. Many times the data published by the agencies vary considerably which confuse the data users. Rain gauges and river gauges are not distributed at block level and panchayat level to generate data for decentralised planning. Also the data are not shared by the various agencies. For example, the data in the Water Year Book prepared by P.W.D. is considered confidential. A coordinated arrangement for data collection has to be brought about through networks.

Location, Area Elevation, etc.

The toposheets prepared by the Surveyor General of India provide valuable informations like location, contour map, important institutions, rivers and roads which are of much use for decentralised planning. Since this map is classified, it is not available for use at the local level. With the development of techniques of remote sensing using satellites and aircrafts, such details regarding any part of the globe has become easily available with the world-wide outlets of NASA. Therefore, possibilities of publication of Maps information which do not affect national security have to be explored.

Meteorological Data

As stated earlier, meteorological data are not available at block and panchayat level for decentralised planning. Valuable meteorological information over a long period of time is available with the plantations of coffee and tea once owned by foreign countries. Pooling of the available data as well as installation of equipments in new areas are needed to generate meteorological data for planning at block and panchayat level. The reliability and quality of meteorological data are to be ensured.

Land-use and Cropping Pattern

Sub-district level data on land-use and cropping pattern are not published. The Department of Economics and Statistics conducts a sample survey every year to estimate land use pattern. But sample size is not adequate to obtain precise estimates at decentralised level.

From 1975-76 to 1986-87 data on land-use and cropping pattern are collected under the centrally-sponsored scheme of Establishment of an Agency for Reporting Agricultural Statistics (EARAS). Under the system 20 per cent of the revenue villages are completely enumerated every year and there by completing all the villages during five years. Every year district-wise data on all crops (for paddy taluk-wise estimate are available) are estimated on the basis of 20 per cent sample. Since all the villages are surveyed completely once in five years village-wise details are available in the village directory maintained in the Directorate of Economics and Statistics. Since the planning units are panchayats and blocks, and the jurisdiction of panchayats and villages are not co-terminus in most cases an early attempt should be made to retabulate the village directories to generate panchayat and block level data.

In view of the importance of data at block level, survey design fc the collection of agricultural statistics has now been revised fror 1987-88 to generate block level data. The practice of complet examination of all the revenue villages once in five years has bee discontinued. It is hoped that block level data on land use pattern cropping pattern, yield rates and production of agricultura commodities will be available soon. If panchayat level data have to b generated the sample sizes will have to be increased considerably Block-wise Data on the number of operational holdings anc agricultural practices are collected through the quinquennial Agricultural Census.

Land-use and cropping pattern according to the 12 agro-climatic zones in the state are not available. This is an important gap in the data for decentralised planning.

The cost of production of important crops is an important gap in the primary agricultural statistics. The data generated on the Cost of Cultivation of paddy and coconut by the Government of India through cost of cultivation unit in Economics Department of University of Kerala is not published. The Economics and Statistics Department conducts studies on cost of cultivation of paddy, coconut, tapioca, arecanut, ginger and turmeric and the data are published. Also data on the marketable surplus of agricultural produce are not available. The area under and production of agricultural commodities are and always under estimated since details of crops cultivated in the large extent of encroached forest lands are not included.

Irrigation Statistics

Estimates of area irrigated by different sources are obtained from the sample surveys conducted by the Economics and Statistics Department. The important data gaps are block-wise and panchayat-wise information on seasonal availability of water, cropping pattern in command areas, cost and return on irrigation projects.

Live-stock

Data on livestock at panchayat and block levels are not published, eventhough available in the Directorate of Animal Husbandry. Data on cost of production of livestock and livestock products, calf mortality and morbidity, consumption of meat and meat products, production and consumption of cattle feed, export and import of livestock products, etc. are not available at panchayat and block levels.

Fishery Statistics

The important data gaps in marine and inland fishing statistics are, fishing village-wise data on catch, price reported on different species of fish, number of fishing vessels and gears, etc. Details of water spread area are not available at panchayat and block level. The quality and reliability of data available are also very poor. The recommendation of the National Commission on Agriculture to conduct census survey of the fishery sector has to implemented.

Forest Statistics

Considerable variations are observed in the total forest area estimated by different agencies. Area under forest reported by the Forest Department and area estimated by remote sensing techniques vary considerably. The important data gaps are details of deforestation and loss due to illegal encroachment and forest fires, collection and removal of forest produce, forest vegetation and environment, etc. Data relating to forestry are to be collected extensively and systematically. The forest statistics available at present are not according to the administrative divisions in the state.

Transport Statistics

Block-wise statistics on roads and motor vehicles are not available. Data on inland water transport and transport by the private sector are inadequate. Traffic surveys are to be conducted to collect data on passenger and goods traffic. Details of inter-block movement of goods are to be collected regularly.

Energy Statistics

The available data on consumption and distribution system for electricity do not conform to administrative divisions. Attempts should be made to reclassify the data according to district, block and panchayats. The availability of data is limited to the supply side. Details like number of pumpsets energised according to horse power, farm size, crops, social group of ownerships, etc. are not available. (It is reported that K.S.E.B. is the only Electricity Board without a statistical unit.) The data on rural energy sources have to be built up systematically.

Trade Statistics

Details of goods traded in the different stations are not available. The data generated in the computer booking system of railways and the data available in check posts can be of some use in decentralised planning.

Industrial Statistics

The Annual Survey of Industries (ASI) covers only the factories registered under the Indian Factories Act. The Economics Census also covers only this category of industries.

The results of ASI are released with a time lag of three to four years. Adhoc surveys like census of small scale industries, census of Handlooms, Survey of coir workers, Raw Material Survey, etc. do not cover industries in unorganised sector and in some cases industries outside the cooperative fold. There is no system for regular flow of data on industrial activities. Also the tabulation and processing of data are to be done block-wise to facilitate decentralised planning. Sample survey on village and small scale industries and industries in unorganised sector are to be conducted regularly. Details like capacity utilisation, production, value added, pattern of investment, employment, etc. are to be collected block-wise.

Educational Statistics

Information on non-formal education, drop-outs, private expenditure on education, socio-economic background of students and teachers, pattern of capital formation in education sector, migration of adducted manpower, availability of infrastructure facilities in educational institutions, etc. are not available for decentralised planning.

Health Statistics

Health statistics relating to the institutions in private sector are not available. The most important data gap in health sector is in respect of morbidity and environmental pollution. To improve the accuracy and quality of data the system of records at the level of primary units may be improved. Vital statistics like birth rates, death rates, life expectancy etc., according to sex, age and social groups are not available at panchayat and block levels.

Housing Statistics

Important details on land less households, rental houses, rates of rent, demand for new houses, etc. are not available for decentralised planning. Data on number of persons living in *kutcha* houses and number of houses which do not have the basic amenities like safe drinking water, sanitation facilities and electricity are not available at block and panchayat level.

Scheduled Castes and Scheduled Tribes

Data in respect of SC/ST relating to nutrition and health standards, land possessed and cultivated, land alienated, wage rates and earnings, etc. are lacking. The age-wise and class-wise distribution of tribal students are not available. Details regarding resources and infrastructure available in the SC habitats and ST settlements, etc. is lacking. Socio-economic surveys are to be conducted before the beginning of five year plans.

Manpower Statistics

Data from various sources like NSSO, Employment department, Directorate of Economics and Statistics, etc. on work force, employment, unemployment, migration, etc. are not comparable. Comprehensive and up to date data on employment are not available for decentralised planning. Details of skills and seasonal unemployment, productivity, etc. are not available at present. Regular surveys may be conducted once in five years.

Prices

The machinery for, prices' collection may be streamlined and number of price aspects like variables on supply side and demand side are to be collected. Appropriate shadow prices may be constructed for planning purposes. Data on important variables like land prices are not collected and published.

Tenancy

The data on area of land according to type of ownership is not available. This is important in the case of Scheduled Tribes who have no right on the forest land they possessed. There is also large scale alienation of tribal land regarding which data are not available.

Women Development

Details regarding the contribution of women to the economy are not quantified. Details regarding the assets, liabilities, income and expenditure patterns are not available even at macro level. Various types of skills possessed by women and its utilisation are not documented. A techno-economic survey to identify skills, resources, potential for development and planning priorities of women is to be done for the preparation of a realistic plan and its effective implementation.

Target Group

The starting point in the decentralised planning for providing minimum needs to be people is identification of the target group. It is necessary to identify families lacking minimum facilities like food, housing, access to drinking water, etc. The efforts made by the Rural Development Department are only to identify beneficiaries for the Integrated Rural Development Programme (IRDP) implemented through blocks. Details of the skills and resources available in the area are needed for the preparation of realistic plans at micro level. Such details are yet to be collected.

Development History

The development history has not been properly documented. The development history at the micro level has to be investigated and documented in order to evolve a plan for sustained development. A study of the historical development of various sectors of the economy will throw light on the constrains of development and on factors which promoted development. A study of success and failures of schemes implemented in the past is of much help for evolving new strategies for planning. The details available with numerous reports like District Gazetteers are helpful to make a beginning to study factors like migration of people, evolution of cultivation practices, development of education and other infrastructure like roads, development of rural skills, attitudes and aptitudes of people, rise and fall of industries and process of environment degradation.

Data Collection

The local level institutions and their potential to generate reliable data relevant for decentralised planning at reduced cost and speed is not tapped. For example, soil testing can be done in the laboratories of schools and colleges and a soil map can be prepared pooling the information collected by the Agricultural Department, Educational Institutions, etc.

It is seen that there is no uniformity in the levels at which data are collected by different agencies in different sectors. Regular arrangements are to be made for the collection and processing of data at panchayat and block levels required for decentralised planning and administration. The present procedure adopted for the collection of data has to be suitably modified for this purpose.

Instead of the present system of conducting surveys on a *ad hoc* basis like housing survey and unemployment survey a bench mark survey at the beginning of a plan period can be conducted ensuring people's participation through involvement of panchayats and voluntary organisations. The expertise of the government departments and manpower of the educated youth can be pooled. This will give a sense of participation in the development process. An action plan for conducting surveys during the intermediate period to study the special problems can also be prepared.

Certification of Data

The data collected from various sources on different occasions must be properly checked and only certified data should be stored in the data bank and used. The person heading the Data Bank should be a good economic analyst with thorough understanding of statistical and econometric techniques. Data measurable on cardinal and ordinal scales are to be processed to help arrive at development decisions. The data should be amenable to mathematical and statistical analysis.

Extent of Data-base

More extensive data and a better information system are necessary for preparation of realistic plans at the decentralised level. In the plan models adopted for decentralised planning, economic and socio-political variables will be considered because the plan formulation takes into account the desire and will of the people, methodology for identification of target groups, time and space dimensions for projects included in the plan etc.

Methodology for Collecting Primary Data

Methodology for collection of primary data is to be decided on the basis of a trade off between cost, speed and reliability of data. For identification of target groups for various assistances and for collection of taxes, census method may have to be adopted, even though it requires more money and time. In case like diagnostic studies to arrive at inference as impact of development schemes, studies to measure the awareness and preference of the people, sample surveys, properly designed and executed, will serve the purpose.

Access to Information

Unwarranted confidentiality should be done away with and data should be made available to all planners and researchers. Wherever confidentiality is absolutely required, relevant data should be converted into case studies. In many cases, the data collection is done after giving an assurance that the information about supplier of data will be kept confidential. This will sometimes restrict the supply of data at micro-level. But without such a guarantee, some items of data could not be generated.

It is difficult to measure with the conventional methods some of the variables such as black-money and trade statistics. In such cases, the feasibility of adopting techniques like Randomised Response Techniques has to be explored.

A good data-base is a prerequisite for planning. But it must be determined exactly *what* (kind of) data are necessary, at what point of time (*when*) and *how* it can be collected at minimum cost and time. By *whom* must it be collected and *where* it should be stored for easy retrieval when necessary, are also important considerations.

For what we see now is quite disturbing. The country has plenty of data at various levels but some of it is quite useless *per se* and by virtue of it's not being available when needed. Many details are collected at the offices at the lowest/most local level and are sent up to the departmental head at the state level — and these statistics fill pages which are never utilised. These are matters determined years ago which probably served a purpose at that time, but not now. With this paper is attached a check list of data that are necessary for district planning. This may have to be adapted according to the need of the moment or the area. So we must distinguish between nice-to-know data and need-to-know data. It may be unbelievable, but there are vested interests insisting on the collection of different types of data, whether these are useful or not. Cutting out the collection of some aspects of data or using computers for storage and retrieval may result in displacement of persons, at least in the transition period and hence insistence of collection of all kinds of data.

Of all aspects, storage and retrieval seem most important. Now, with modern technology and the ambitious plans for linking, through a nation-wide computer network from the District to the State, to the Union, full facilities would be available for getting the information when you want it or need it, anywhere. This requires that people at all levels must be trained to be facile with computers: programming, feeding and retrieval. This will prevent the enormous waste in keeping the District machines idle and useless, and eating up space and energy in the office.

Many people engaged in this task of data collection for district planning want to achieve perfection and prepare an enormous schedule of time and energy for putting together the data. Sometimes the "ideal" is the enemy of action. We have to plunge into the water to facilitate the process of learning to swim and not wait until we are master of the art. It must be remembered that collecting data are not a one-time matter and that existing data must be adjusted/updated/modified, etc. throughout the district planning process, from time to time.

CHECK LIST OF DATA-BASE FOR DECENTRALISED PLANNING

National Resources

1. Location

Location of the area as indicated by

(i) northern latitude and eastern longitudes
(ii) regions bound by:

2. Geographical area of the district according to

(i) taluks and villages
(ii) blocks and panchayats, municipal corporations and Municipalities
(iii) natural division — Low land, mid land and high land
(iv) maps showing the above details.

3. Soil

(i) Soil types at block/panchayat level
(ii) Soil capability at block/panchayat level
(iii) Area prone to soil erosion
(iv) Map showing the above details

4. Meteorological details at block level like

(i) Monthly rainfall (actual and normal)
(ii) temperature (maximum and minimum)
(iii) relative humidity and
(iv) special weather phenomena

5. Water Resources

Surface water

(i) Monthly run off according to river basins/watersheds

(ii) Number of tanks with water spread area

Groundwater

(iii) Groundwater potential — areas suitable for digging bore wells/tube wells and open draw wells.
(iv) Number of wells and tube wells, bore wells
(v) Number of pump sets
(vi) Maps showing the above details

6. Mineral resources available for economic utilisation.

(i) Maps

7. Environmental setting

(i) Area prone to floods, droughts, saline intrusion, land slide, etc.
(ii) Map showing above details

8. Land utilisation pattern

(i) Area under forests, land put to non-agricultural uses, barren and uncultivable land, pastures, land under miscellaneous tree crops, cultivable waste, fallow land, current fallow, net area sown, area sown more than once and total cropped area.

9. Land-holding pattern

(i) number or operational holdings and area operated according to size class (marginal, small, semi-medium, medium and large), ownership of land.

10. Cropping pattern

(i) Area under important crops
(ii) Production of important crops
(iii) Productivity of important crops
(iv) Area under high-yielding varieties
(v) Net Area irrigated source-wise
(vi) Gross area irrigated crop-wise and source-wise

(vii) Consumption of fertilizers — Session-wise, nutrient-wise and crop-wise
(viii) Index of cropping intensity
(ix) Cost of cultivation — crop-wise
(x) Agriculture implements and machineries

11. Livestock population according to

(i) category; and
(ii) genetic variety
(iii) veterinary institutions and milk cooperatives
(iv) production and productivity of milk, egg, meat, etc.
(v) disease pattern of livestock
(vi) fish production, landing centres
(vii) population engaged in fishing
(viii) forest produces
(ix) wild-life sanctuaries and tourist centres.

Human Resources

1. Population and population density according to

(i) administrative divisions
(ii) natural divisions of geographical area
(iii) sex
(iv) rural and urban areas
(v) social groups like S.C. and S.T.
(vi) religion and
(vii) age
(viii) ST and SC habitats with infrastructure details

2. Literacy rate according to

(i) administrative divisions
(ii) sex
(iii) rural-urban regions
(iv) social groups like SC/ST

3. Number of households according to language spoken in the household.

4. Important vital rates like age specific birth rates and death rates, fertility indices, labour forces.
5. Main workers, marginal workers and non-workers.

   (i) Main workers according to industrial category (like cultivators, agricultural labours) and sex

6. Population estimates according to age, between census years.
7. Population projections, according to age up to 2005 AD.
8. Employment in organised sectors in private and government according to industry division and according to sex.
9. Employment in unorganised sector according to skill, sex, social groups, etc.
10. Employment seekers registered in the employment exchanges according to

    (i) level of education
    (ii) occupational classification
    (iii) professional and technical qualification
    (iv) sex
    (v) waiting time

11. Block-wise number of agricultural labourers.
12. Number of other rural labourers.
13. Average daily wage according to

    (i) skill
    (ii) sex
    (iii) occupation

14. Block-wise number of households below poverty line according to

    (i) Social group
    (ii) Employment status

15. Number of disabled persons according to type of disability.
16. Emigration and Immigration of labour.
17. Labour training facilities. Wage rates according to sex and activity.

Financial Resources

1. Financial Institutions:

   (i) Number of commercial banks with their service areas/Number of cooperative credit societies
   (ii) Other financial institutions like K.F.C. and Chit funds Amount of deposits received, advances provided, over dues, etc.

2. District Income:

   (i) Net domestic product at constant and current price according to industry of origin.

Economic Infrastructure

1. Transport and Communication:

   (i) Length of roads according to

      (a) agencies maintaining like P.W.D. and panchayats
      (b) type of surface

   (ii) Length of railway line/distance from railway line
   (iii) Airport or distance from airport
   (iv) Harbours or distance from harbours
   (v) Number of post offices, public telephones booths, telegraph offices
   (vi) Number of motor vehicles according to different categories
   (vii) Number of accidents.

2. Markets

   (i) Number of wholesale and retail ration depots, maveli stores, cooperative stores, etc. for Public Distribution System.
   (ii) Number of regulated markets, markets and number of shops.

3.Power

   (i) electricity generated, number of sub-stations, length of low tension lines.

(ii) Number of different categories of consumers and power consumption.

(iii) Sources of non-conventional energy generated — number of micro power projects, bio-gas plants, etc.

Social Infrastructure

1. Education

(i) Number of schools (Government and Private)

(ii) Number of students (sex-wise) and number of teachers under pre-primary, lower primary, upper primary and high schools.

(iii) List of schools lacking basic amenities like safe drinking water, electricity, libraries and sanitation facilities.

(iv) Course-wise intake of students under different institutions for technical/vocational institutions. Details of infrastructure lacking in these institutions.

2. Housing

(i) Number of old, dilapidated houses and huts.

(ii) Number of houses according to availability of basic facilities like electricity, water sealed lavatories and drinking water.

3. Health:

(i) Number of private and government medical institutions, bed strength and specialities under allopathic, ayurvedic and homeopathic systems.

(ii) Month-wise number of patients treated in the above institutions.

(iii) Disease pattern.

(iv) Number of doctors and paramedical staff working in the institutions.

4. List of defunct cooperative institutions.
5. List of sick industrial units.
6. List of voluntary organisations engaged in development/welfare activities with their area of professionalisation.

9

DATA DISCREPANCY AND PLANNING ANOMALY

Milindo Chakravarti and Amitava Mukherjee

I

Irrespective of the size of the planning unit, i.e. national regional or local, a planning process has two district categories, one, formulation of plan proposals and two, the plan-prescriptions are to be implemented within a specified time frame. Here, we shall confine ourselves to the discussion on the first step only, i.e. formulation of plan proposals and for convenience of exposition, we shall restrict our discussion to one level of a decentralised planning set up, viz., at the block level.

Broadly, in the process of plan proposal formulation four sub-steps can be identified. They are:

(i) Data collection and analysis of the present condition of the area;
(ii) Projections of future conditions;
(iii) Formulation of a policy/strategies; and
(iv) Preparation of action plans/projects.

Table 9.1 that follows gives a summary picture of the several steps involved in formulating the plan proposals.[1]

It is apparent that the stepping stone necessary for future perspective planning is a thorough knowledge about the present condition pertaining to the areal unit under consideration of the planners. Indeed, it may be argued in this context that one of the compulsions of shift towards decentralised mode of planning from the earlier centralised pattern in many developing countries is the fact that the information regarding ground situation from all the nooks and corners of a country can be best understood at the scene of action, and as a consequence proper planning prescriptions could be formulated by planner who has locate near the scene of action. Thus decentralised planning at block levels may be deemed to have been initiated mainly with the hope that correct and updated block-level information data-base will be available with the Panchayat organisations and local-level officers, who, as a result will be able to formulate proper plan proposals in the light of such available information.

TABLE 9.1: Five Category Analysis Conductive to Four Step Planning

I. Step-A

Data Collection analysis of the present conditions of the area.

(a) A-I External conditions and their relationship to the area.
(b) A-2 Characteristics of the area.
(c) A-3 Pattern of activities of the people as the results of A-I & A-2.
(d) A-4 outputs, products or working accomplished resulting from the above activities.
(e) A-5 Consequences of the uses being made of the above outputs.

II. Step-B

Projections of future conditions.

(a) B-I Forecasts of future changes in A-I.
(b) B-2 Assess the reaction of A-2 against B-I.
(c) B-3 Projects the pattern of activities, based on A-3 and B-2.
(d) B-4 Estimate the future outputs of the area based on A-4 and B-3.
(e) B-5 Foresee the consequences from A-5 and B-4.

III. Step-C

Formation of a policy/strategies.

(a) C-I Determining what development at the local level is necessary in the context of changes in the external conditions.
(b) C-2 Determining what changes of areal characteristic is necessary to realize the expected pattern of activities (strategy objectives).
(c) C-3 Determining what pattern of activities is necessary to realize the expected outputs (development objectives).
(d) C-4 Determining what output of the area must be expected in order to realize the needed consequences (plan objectives/targets).
(e) C-5 Determining what consequences are necessary to attain the goals of local development (policy objectives).

IV. Step-D

Preparation of Action plans/Projects.

(a) D-I Assessment of possible government supports for local development.
(b) D-2 Project identification and objectives setting.
(c) D-3 Designing proposed work components of the project.
(d) D-4 Determine the size and site of the work components of the project.
(e) D-5 Justification of the project.

II

The present paper attempts to examine the quality of the existing data-base in respect of the three districts, namely, Cooch Behar, Jalpaiguri and Darjeeling of the State of West Bengal, which presents a successful model of decentralised planning. Because it is not possible to discuss all the factors of information-data-base universe necessary for planning process here, we would concentrate on the data base pertaining to two most necessary elements of that information-data-base universe, namely, (i) number of inhabited village and (ii) population. In the context of examining the quality of existing data-base we shall refer to two sources, (a) Primary Census Abstracts (PCA) of the respective districts (1981 series) and (b) Annual Action Plan (AAP) prepared by the concerned Lead Bank of the respective districts. The reason behind considering information from AAP is that it is or it ought to be also a part of the District Plan exercise undertaken by the district planning authority.

One need not labour the point that information about the characteristics of the concerned area is of basic importance while there is an attempt to formulate a plan. Further, development blocks, which is favoured by many experts as the most appropriate planning units,[2] are constituted of certain number of villages, and towns. As a consequences, the block-level planners must know the correct number of inhabited villages and towns falling within the jurisdiction of the concerned blocks. The data that are available regarding the number of villages in the three districts mentioned earlier from AAP and PCA are given in Tables 9.2 to 9.5.

Tables 9.2 to 9.5 indicate that since the introduction of decentralised planning in 1985, there has been no change in the number of inhabited villages either in Cooch Behar or in Darjeeling, while there has been a considerable fall in the number of inhibited villages in

Jalpaiguri during the period 1985-88. In fact AAP 1987 also gives the same figures as provided in AAP 1985 in respect of the block-wise distribution of inhabited villages. Thus we are left with a situation in which within a span of one year 71 villages in the district have either been redesigned or vanished or been abandoned by its residents.

TABLE 9.2: Blockwise Distribution of Inhabited Villages in Cooch Behar District

Block	As per AAP 1985	As per AAP 1987
Cooch Behar-I	141	141
Cooch Behar-II	116	116
Dinhata-I	130	130
Dinhata-II	116	116
Sitai	053	053
Mathabhanga-I	102	102
Mathabhanga-II	093	093
Sitalkuchi	067	067
Tufanganj	127	127
Mekligant	140	140
Haldibari	059	059
Total	1144	1144

TABLE 9.3: Blockwise Distribution of Inhabited Villages in Jalpaiguri District.

Block	As per AAP 1985	+ As per AAP 1988
Jalpaigur (Sadar)	129	129
Rajaunge	099	099
Maynaguri	090	090
Dhupguri	108	108
Malbazar	107	107
Meteli	031	031
Nagrakata	033	033
Alipurduar-I	059	045
Alipurduar-II	080	076
Falakata	064	064
Kumargram	056	042
Madarihat	050	032
Kalchini	047	018
Total	947	876

TABLE 9.4: Blockwise Distribution of Inhabited Villages in Darjeeling District

Blocks	As per AAP 1985	As per AAP 1988
Kharibari-Phansidewa	485	285
Siliguri-Naxalbari	222	222
Kurseong	064	064
Mirik	013	013
Jorebungalow-Sukhipokhri	081	081
Rangli-Rangliot	020	020
Darjeeling-Poolbazar	081	081
Kalimpong-I	028	028
Kalimpong-II	070	070
Gorubathan	036	036
Total	1100	1100

Let us now consider the PCA 1981 data that are presented in Table 9.5.

TABLE 9.5: Number of Villages as per 1981 Census

District	Inhabited	Uninhabited	Total
Cooch Behar	1139	29	1168
Jalpaiguri	0736	20	0756
Darjeeling	0759	51	0710

A comparison of the AAP statistical information with that provided in PCA is somewhat confusing. In case of all the districts AAP figures relating to the number of inhabited villages come out to be overestimates of PCA figures. The extent of overestimation is marginal in case of Cooch Behar (1144–1139=5) but considerable in the context of Jalpaiguri (876–736=140) and very high for Darjeeling (1100–659=541).

The population figures are somewhat more confusing. Table 9.6 through Table 9.8 provide blockwise population estimates for the three districts under consideration as provided in the respective AAP's.

The Census figures as obtained from PCA 1981 are given in Table 9.9.

TABLE 9.6: Blockwise Distribution of Population in Cooch Behar District

Block	Total Population
Cooch Behar-I	265142
Cooch Behar-II	202911
Dinhata-I	195374
Dinhata-II	157516
Sitai	069395
Mathabhanga-I	155107
Mathabhanga-II	135105
Sitalkuchi	125634
Tufanganj	288235
Mekligant	103190
Haldibari	073993
Total	1771562

TABLE 9.7: Blockwise Distribution of Population in Jalpaiguri District.

Block	Total Population
Jalpaigur (Sadar)	266022
Rajaunge	196388
Maynaguri	199002
Dhupguri	144646
Malbazar	203850
Meteli	074334
Nagrakata	069890
Alipurduar-I	179256
Alipurduar-II	152907
Falakata	167072
Kumargram	121781
Madarihat	052982
Kalchini	167590
Total	1995721

In the context of population figures, thc AAP figures are seemingly underestimates of PCA figures. The extent of underestimation is very nominal in case of Cooch Behar district (1771643–1771562=81), but astonishingly high for Jalpaiguri district (221487–1995721=219150). Darjeeling comes in between the boundary of under-estimation provided by these two districts with (1024269–1006925=17844) about eighteen thousand people remaining unrecognised and unaccounted for by the AAP.

Thus the existing information data-base provides us to choose between two alternatives. The first alternative is to accept the AAP figures, where there are comparatively more inhabited villages and less population than the second alternative in the form of PCA figures where we have comparatively less inhabited villages and more population.

TABLE 9.8: Blockwise Distribution of Population in Darjeeling District

Block	Total Population
Kharibari-Phansidewa	157033
Siliguri-Naxalbari	303378
Kurseong	081558
Mirik	029270
Jorebungalow-Sukhipokhri	080439
Rangli-Rangliot	051318
Darjeeling-Poolbazar	147645
Kalimpong-I	075179
Kalimpong-II	041926
Gorubathan	038868
Total	1006425

TABLE 9.9: Total District Population as per PCA 1981

District	Total Population
Cooch Behar	1771643
Jalpaiguri	2214871
Darjeeling	1024269

In formulating development plans the estimate of average population per village, plays the role of a good index in making several decisions, say for example, creation of drinking water sources, establishment of schools etc.. Table 9.10 provides the estimates of average population per inhabited village in the district sunder consideration as obtained from the AAP's and PCA.

TABLE 9.10: Average Population per Inhabited Village

District	As per AAP	As per PCA
Cooch Behar	1458.57	1555.44
Jalpaiguri	2278.22	3009.34
Darjeeling	914.93	1554.28

III

The impact of such an informational discrepancy on the planning process can be examined in several contexts but we consider it in the context of the service area approach to each of the functioning commercial bank branches. The district level lead banks were required to adopt a system of assigning specific areas to each bank branch which it can concentrate on the productive lending and to the development of the area, a view that was further endorsed by both banks and Economists. Each bank branch, under this approach, will have a designated service area, which involves five distinct steps in its implementation. They are:

(i) identification of the service area for each bank branch;
(ii) survey of the villages of the service area for assessing the potential beneficiaries;
(iii) preparation of credit plans on an annual basis for the service are by the bank branch;
(iv) co-ordination between credit institutions on the one hand and field level development agencies on the other on an on-going basis for the effective implementation of credit plans.
(v) a continuous system of monitoring the progress in the implementation of the plans and individual schemes.

The details are given in Annexure I.

Thus, the first step of the new approach was to allocate specific areas to all the rural and semi-urban branches of commercial banks and regional rural banks, with each bank looking after 15-25 villages. The actual number of inhabited villages in all the districts under consideration, being different in different data sources the process of identification of service areas for the bank branches was not accurate. In case of the AAP estimates being correct and the service areas being earmarked on the basis of PCA estimates, the branches will be left with need to cater more villages, than they should actually be allocated. On the other hand, if it is the other way round, the branches will have a smaller area to cover, than it was anticipated and as a result the overhead establishment cost will be higher, which would aggravate the loss position of the rural branches of the commercial banks. Additionally this would generate almost intractable problems for the branches, causing serious confusions. While one bank, say Bank 'A' would proceed on the assumption that a village, say village 'X' is to be serviced by Bank 'B', Bank 'B' will not service village 'X' because, it may actually be beyond its territory *de facto*, though dejure it may seemingly be under its purview. The possibility, therefore, lurks that with weak data-bases there could be considerable areas which would go un-attended, though they need the most attention of development agencies including the banks.

The task of assigning specific number of villages, therefore, to every branch cannot be done correctly in the districts under consideration in view of the discrepancies in the existing information data-base. To circumvent this difficulty, an alternative approach may be of fixing a specific population to be catered to by a bank branch, where also we run into problems, in view of the discrepancy in the existing information-data-base. If AAP estimates are followed, with the other (PAC) estimate being correct, the branches will have to cater to a larger population than it was originally assigned and find problems in servicing the area properly. On the other hand, if the PCA estimates are followed, with the AAP estimates being correct, operational cost of the branches will be higher than the optimum, which is contrary to the basic rationale behind a planning process. The banks are already under fire for their low profitability. If the planning process is grounded on foundations that cause a hike in operational cost of the banks, it is going to make further in roads into the already weak profitability conditions of the banks. This is hardly a desirable position.

The object of Service Area approach to Credit Plan formulation being clearly to effect an equitable development, it is to be an integral part of the entire decentralised planning process. However, the haste with which it has been part across, basing it on weak data-base, is likely to produce more confusion than development. This is particularly true because the information base is heavily biased in favour of the agricultural sector, to the neglect of industry. It is true that the rural areas depend heavily on agriculture but it is nevertheless as much true that total neglect of industry may lead to serve problems of an altogether different gainer. It would be wise to set in motion corrective steps early.

There are other problems in this regard, the foremost amongst which is the choice of *unit of survey*. The surveys are to be carried out on the basis 'mouzas', listed in the 1981 Census reports. In West Bengal the'Panchayati Raj' has taken a firm root so much so that planning has been decentralised up to the Gram Panchayat level. Thus, the Panchayat level information are available with the territory covered by gram panchayats being taken as the units, and in many cases, the "mouza" boundaries and the "gram panchayat" boundaries are not co-terminous. Indeed there are gram panchayats which are divided into two mouzas. Thus when the information are to be collected on a "mouza basis", the gram panchayat level information are distributed between the mouzas assuming equal concentration of the concerned variable either in respect of population or in respect of geographical area. This assumption of equal concentration can hardly be tenable when information is being collected at a micro-level.

There exists confusion with regard to the specification of the source of information. For several subjects, more than one sources have been indicated. For example, for the population figures, information are to be collected from Census Reports (1981) as well as the concerned from the gram panchayats; with regard to the information regarding agricultural labours, banks have been advised to consult the 'Census Report' (1981) along with the information available with Agricultural Extension Officers. This approach totally neglects the reality that whenever different agencies are involved for providing or collecting, information, markedly different quantitative values can emerge. This possibility is made manifest by a comparison of the population figures available in the Census Report and that available from the Gram Panchayats. If the population figures of all the Gram Panchayats of Jalpaiguri District (as provided by the concerned Gram Panchayats) are added up, it comes out to be 19,95,721 in 1981 whereas the population of the district as per 1981 Census Report is 22,14,871. Thus possibility of confusions abounding in consulting different sources for information with regard to any variable, cannot be ruled out. It is very real.

The content of the schedule of informations to be collected also leaves much to be desired. A thorough glance over the 22 items listed reveals two important characteristics, namely:

(a) information of every description regarding agricultural potential of the village are to be collected; and

(b) information regarding industrial potential of the area is deemed almost redundant, and whenever required, it seemingly is only *obiter dicta* (loosely speaking) to information regarding agricultural activity.

Let us look at item No. 3 Facilities Available. In all 19 facilities have been listed. Of them not a single relates to the availability of industrial facilities proper. Even though facilities like railway station, petrol pumps, and extent of electrification, have been listed, the majority of the information on facilities available relates to such subjects agricultural assistant, agro-service centre, dairy society, poultry society, veterinary aid centre, artificial insemination centre etc., which leads to the inference that the information required to be collected, such as with regard to railways and petrol pumps, are mainly in relation to emphasising thrust on agricultural sector.

Indeed most of the information sought to be collected are directly related to agriculture except one, namely, item number 20, which concerned with industrial activities, where the information sought regarding the number of handlooms, number of silk textiles units etc., are indicative of the planners being only seemingly interested in the number of different artisan units obtaining in the concerned village. Curiously enough the schedule seeks no information about the quantity of input requirements by such artisan units; available sources of inputs in the vicinity of the village; the marketing facilities existing in respect of both the inputs and outputs; input mix; cost of production and profit margin per unit of output, though all these information have been sought in respect of the agricultural sector.

Thus the points that emerge quite clearly from the activities under 'Service Area Approach' are :

(a) Even though the importance of having an information data-base at the village level, has been realised, the planners seem to be happy with mere compilation of facts available from several secondary sources, which has the potential of creating confusion within the banking system.

(b) The planners seem to have been dissatisfied with the existing practice of people's active participation in development programmes, thus reinstating the responsibility of identifying the beneficiaries on the bank-officials who are accountable only to their superiors.

IV

We started our exercise with an eye on the decentralised planning process introduced by the government of West Bengal since 1985-86. Since, as we have noted earlier, the AAP's ought to be also parts of district plan document and on the other hand, information in the AAP's are mainly collected from block level plan documents, the block and district level planning activities initiated by the state government are also prone to be highly affected by the existing apparent inconsistencies in the information-data-base. Shall we say then that decentralised planning to be successful, with such discrepancies about the quantum of available human resources and their agglomeration in the form of village-settlements still not being solved, has a long struggle ahead of it. And if district Credit Plans one to form part of District Plans, or be dovetailed to District Plans, then the current method of implementing the "Service Area Approach" requires substantive changes. But fortunately this is not a difficult task.

NOTES

1. Misra, R.P. (edited) (1983): *Local Level Planning and Development* (New Delhi: Sterling Publishers Private Limited), p.288.
2. We are not joining issue to the continuing debate on block Vs district as proper unit of planning in a process of planning form below.
3. Reserve Bank of India: *Service Area Approach Formulation of Credit Plan* (Bombay: Rural Planning and Credit Department, Central Office), May 1988.

ANNEXURE I

Service Area Approach — Salient Feature*

The Service Area Approach involves five major aspects which are s follows:

(a) Identification and allocation of service area for each bank branch
(b) Survey of villages in the service area for assessing the potential for lending activities and identification of beneficiaries for assistance
(c) Preparation of credit plan on an annual basis for the service area by each branch
(d) Coordination between credit institutions on the one hand and field level development agencies on the other on an on-ging basis for the effective implementation of the credit plans, and
(e) System of continuous monitoring of progress in the implementation of the plans.

Items at (a) to (c) and the aspects are elaborated below. Guidelines egarding items (d) and (e) above are to be issued separately

a) Identification and Allocation of Service Area

Specific areas will be identified and allocated to each rural and emi-urban branch of commercial banks including the Regional Rural Banks. Each branch may have approximately 15 to 25 village under its rea of operation, which will be known as its Service Area. Cluster pproach would be followed in selecting the villages for service area, heir contiguity and proximity to the branch being the other main riteria. Village in the same Gram Panchayat would, as far as possible, e allotted to the same branch. When a particular village qualifies for llotment to more than one branch on the above principles, allotment may be made to the branch which has the dominant share in financing

* Source: Reserve Bank of India: *Service Area Approach Formulation of Credit Plan* (Bombay : Rural Planning and Credit Department, Central Office) May 1988.

in that village in terms of number of accounts. Subject to the abov criteria, the existing allocation of villages to different branches for th purpose of implementation of IRDP may also be kept in view whil designating areas to different bank branches.

All the villages in the block will have to be allotted among th branches. Banks have been advised to expedite the opening of branche at rural and and semi-urban centres for which allotments have bee made. The State Governments have also been requested to exten necessary assistance to facilitate opening of branches at the allotte identified centres. Opening of the new branches may be completed b December 1988. The service area of the branches, the existin branches covering these villages may take up preparation of villag profiles and transfer such profiles to the new branch as soon as it i opened.

(b) Survey of Villages

After fixation of the service area, each branch is to undertake survey of the allotted villages and prepare village profiles. Such surve will cover different aspects such as existing economic activities an potentialities for their expansion as also for undertaking new activities available infrastructure in the area, existing skills of the villagers an coverage of rural families by the credit institutions, etc. An illustrativ proforma for the survey is given in the annexure to the circular lette date 14 March 1988 appended herewith. It may be noted that what i envisaged is a detailed profile of the village and not a househol survey.

The data available with other agencies such as DRDA, DIC, Bloc and other government departments should be made use of for th purpose of survey. Village-wise survey is expected to be complete within four month from the date of finalisation of service areas.

The village profile thus prepared will have to be update periodically, say once in a year for preparing the credit plans taking into account the developmental changes etc., which have taken place i the interregnum. The branch managers are required to keep themselve abreast of developments taking place in their service area by means by periodical visits to the villages and establishing a continuous contac with the extension and developmental agencies.

(c) Preparation of Credit Plan

Each branch would prepare annual credit plan for its *own service area* on an on-going basis. For this purpose the credit plan will be first prepared for each village and the village credit plans aggregated to from the service area credit plan of the branch. The credit plan should reflect both the needs and the potentialities of the area, on the basis of the information gained through the survey as also other available information from local development agencies such as block authorities and officials connected with agriculture, animal husbandry, irrigation, small scale industry, V.L.W. and Village Panchayat etc. The resources available for meeting the credit plan by way of deposits, including additional deposits to be mobilised, within the service area and the funds that could be obtained from Head Office should also be kept in view in finalising the plan. The Lead Bank Officer has a crucial role in this regard. He should provide necessary guidance and support to all the branch managers in the district in the following areas:

(i) making available information obtained from concerned District Authorities and other agencies regarding likely developments in infrastructure and supporting services for different activities in the near future in the are of the branch and special programmes to be taken up.

(ii) making available standard schemes for guidance of Branch Managers covering, among others, the economics of different activities identified as suitable for the district, incorporating therein the economic unit, unit cost, repayment period etc., the availability of refinance facilities from IDBI, NABARD as well as subsidy, if any from Government and other agencies etc.. While preparing the credit plans, branches may keep in view the existing DCP/AAP and identify suitable schemes for financing in their service area. The branch managers should use their own judgement in the light of the first hand information from village surveys as also other information available to them indicating the activities to be financed and the number of units to be financed. The state sponsored programmes such as Integrated Rural Development Programme (IRDP), Self Employment for Educated Unemployed Youth (SEEUY) and Self-employment Programme for Urban Poor (SEPUP) will continue to be handled as hitherto. The targets under such programmes will form part of each branch's credit plan.

The annual credit plans prepared by all the branches in a block together with the lending programmes of the co-operatives, would b consolidated into the Block Credit Plan. This work would be done b the main branch of the lead bank in the block. In exceptional case where the lead bank may not have a branch at the block level, the wor of consolidation of branch credit plans into block credit plans could b done by another bank which has the maximum presence in the block with the assistance and guidance of the lead bank. The lead ban should designate the name of the bank which will perform this task The block plans in turn would be aggregated to form the annua credited plan for the district.

(d) Co-ordination and Monitoring

A Block-level Bankers' Committee (BLBC) would be formed to coordinate the activities of the banks and the government officials. Al the banks operating in the block, including DCCB, LDB and RRE would be members of this committee. In addition, the Block Development Officer and the technical officers in block looking after agriculture, industries, animal husbandry etc., would also be the members. The Lead Bank Officer of the concerned district would be the Chairman of the Committee, and in his absence, the seniormost branch manager of the lead bank would preside over the meeting and he would also work as its convenor. If the Lead Bank has no branch in the block, as stated earlier, another bank which has maximum presence in the block and designated by the Lead Bank shall act as the convenor. The Lead District Officer of the Reserve Bank of India and the concerned officer from NABARD should draw up definite programmes for attending the block level meeting in such a manner that as many meeting as possible are attended by atleast one of them.

ANNEXURE II

Village Survey-Collection of Data and its Interpretation

As mentioned earlier, proforma for Village Survey has been included in this Annexure. This part contains the information relating to various sources of data collection and is intended to serve as a general guidance to the Branch Manager. Besides these sources, the branch manager may also have to tap other appropriate sources also based upon his personal knowledge. The precise interpretation of each item of data has been elaborated in the following pages. In a nutshell, this is expected to give a clear idea to the Branch Manager as to how the should go about collecting and using the information in the Village Survey Proforma.

SOURCE, USES AND INTERPRETATION OF DATA

Items	Sources		Uses & Interpretation
Name of village: Revenue Circle No.: Panchayat Samiti/Block:	Branch: District:		
1. Distance from the Branch (km)			
2. Is the village accessible throughout the year? (Please (indicate whether the (village is connected by *pucca* roads and the nature of transport facilities available).			
3. Facilities available	Whether located in the village covered	If not, nearest place where available and distance	To be studied with reference to their general adequacy for assessing availability of essential services and infrastructural facilities.

1	2		3
Railway Station	Yes/No	Personal knowledge and local enquiries	Indicates the general level of development of the village
Police Outpost/ Chauki	Yes/No		
Post Office	Yes/No		
Telegraph Office	Yes/No		
Telephone Office	Yes/No		
High School	Yes/No		
Medical Dispensary	Yes/No		
Gram Panchayat	Yes/No		
Gram Sevak	Yes/No		
Agricultural Assistant	Yes/No		
Agro-Service Centre	Yes/No	Personal knowledge and local enquiries	Indicates availability of various types of agricultural inputs and farm equipment(on hire) and also guarantees about their future availability.
Custom-Service Unit	Yes/No		
Dairy Society	Yes/No		Organised outlets for marketing the produce
Poultry Society	Yes/No		
Veterinary Aid Centre	Yes/No		Availability (present and future) of veterinary care for dairy, poultry, sheep rearing, piggery, etc.
Artificial Insemination centre	Yes/No		Availability of good quality animals for dairy scheme.
Outlets for oil & Petroleum (Petrol Pump)			Adequacy of fuel or diesel for pumpsets, tractor, power tillers etc.

1	2	3
Is the village electrified	Yes/No	An important infrastructural facility and constraint as well, determining the scope for industries and irrigation
No. of households electrified No. of Pumpsets energised	Gram Panchayat	
4.(i) a. Total Population Men Women Children Total	(i) Census Data (ii) Gram Panchayat	One of the factors (influencing quantum of credit flow to the village, Gives general idea about workforce, size of women target group under IRDP, DWCRA, etc.
4.(i) b. Of which— Scheduled Castes Scheduled Tribes		Size of this group for credit allocation under programmes like IRDB, SEEUY, SEPUP etc.
c. Literate Persons		Indicator of general awareness reflecting on acceptability of (innovative ideas and schemes.
d. Total No. of households		Size of the village.
(ii) a. Cultivators	(i) Census Data	Occupational pattern of village reflecting general scope for credit to the different sectors e.g., more of landless labour indicates greater emphasis to be given to non-land

1	2	3
		based activities (in preparing the pla
b. Agricultural labourers	(ii) Agricultural Extn. Officers/Agricultural Assistants	
c. Other workers engaged in allied activities such as livestock, fishery, plantation, orchards, etc.	(iii) Industries Promotion/ Extn. Officer	
d. Others engaged in manufacturing, servicing, repairs, transport, storage, fabrication, etc.	(iv) Block Office	
e. Non-workers.		
(iii) No. of households (identified as falling below the poverty line	(i) B D O (ii) Gram Sevak	IRDP target group covered so far and magnitude of future task-factor deciding extent of special concentration required in future.
Out of whom, no. assisted under IRDP		
5. Classification of land holdings 0 to 1 hectare 1 to 2 hectare 2 to 4 hectares Above 4 hectares Total of which under High Yielding Varieties — No. — Area in hectare	(i) Agriculture Extn. officer at block level (ii) Agricultural Assistant/ Village Agriculture Worker(VAW)	Indicates (i) the structure of aggrarian economy (ii) general level of development (presently) (iii) level of extension efforts needed (iv) Scope of crop loan activity (v) extent of need for preparing

1	2			3
				different types of non-farm schemes for small and marginal farmers.
6. A. Sources of Irrigation (i) Tube wells	No.	Area under command	(i) Agrl.Extn. officer at block level	(i) Extent of Irrigation through different sources
(ii) Dug Wells: Not used for irrigation			(ii) Minor Irrigation Department	(ii) influences cropping pattern and intensity — determining demand for crop loan activity.
Used for irrigation			(iii) Agricultural Assistant/VAW	(iii) level of unutilised irrigation facilities
Dugwells in use for Irrigation with: a) Mhots b) Oil engines c) Electric Motors				
(iii) Tanks/precolation tanks				
(iv) Cultivators using lifts on rivers/streams (a) Perennial (b) Seasonal				
(v) Canal Irrigation				
(vi) Irrigation potential created but nct utilised				
B. Irrigation Potential (Future) New Wells			(i) Groundwater survey	(i) Facilities formulation of schemes for development of irrigation.

1	2		3
Lift Irrigation		(ii) Agrl. Extn. Officer at block level	(ii) Scope for modernisation and development of agriculture.
Any scheme to extend flow of irrigation in near future (details regarding availability of groundwater survey reports and their findings, if available)		(iii) Minor irrigation Department	(iii) Scope for credit to minor irrigation activities and crop loan
7. Soil types: Black soils Medium soils		(i) Agriculture Extn. Officer at Block level (ii) Agricultural Assistant/VAW	Determines the type of crop being grown also those which can be cultivated in future.
8. Drainage	Good/Fair/ Bad	Local enquiries	Factor influencing cropping pattern
9. Special Development Programmes	Whether Yes or No		
(i) Tribal Sub-Plan (ii) Special drought prone area projects		(i) BDO (ii) Agrl. Extn. Officer at Block Level	(i) Nature and focus of present development programmes (ii) Further scope for introduction of additional programmes
(iii) Special Rice Production programme		(iii) Irrigation Deptt.	(iii) Cognizance of (i) and (ii) while preparing credit plan for the village
(iv) Special projects for pulses/oilseeds/dairy/ fishery development level		(iv) Veterinary/ Animal Husbandry Deptt. at block level	
(v) Other Agricultural Development Programmes		(v) Lead Bank Officer	

1	2		3
(vi) Ayacut Development Programme		(vi) D.I.C. Officer at Block level	
(vii) Bunding works		(vii) Agricultural Assistant/VAW	
(viii) Dry farming works		(viii) Gram Panchayat	
(ix) SEEUY			
(x) Forestry			
(xi) Wasterland Development			
(xii) Sericulture			
(xiii) Any others (specify)			
(a) Whether the area is susceptible to any long term endemic problems such as:	Whether Yes or No	(i) Local inquiry (ii) B.D.O. (iii) Agrl. Extn. Officer at block level	Understanding nature of calamities Helps to think about provision of credit for the same, if necessary
(i) droughts (ii) floods (iii) sporadic animal diseases (iv) crop pests and diseases		(iv) Veterinary/ Animal Husbandry deptt. at block level (v) Gram Panchayat (vi) Agricultural Assistant/VAW	Helps in selection of scheme/activities with full awareness about pitfalls involved.
(b) If so, give details of such natural calamities, if any, during last 5 years.			
(c) Mention measures taken to overcome the above problems and by whom			
10. Details of the working of village credit societies:		Concerned credit society	Focuses on various dimensions of functioning of cooperative credit society-reflection on the efficiency of society's working as a financing agency
(a) Working of dormant (b) Number of members (c) Number of borrowing members and total area covered			
(d) Whether all eligible members in the area of operation actually covered			Extent and nature of scope left out for the

1	2	3
(e) Percentage of recovery to demand (f) Whether having paid secretary or not (g) Level of credit disbursed during last three years (h) Particulars of revenue recovery proceedings initiated in last three years (i) Drought relief work		branch for its credit activity.
11. Nearest market centre (Distance from the (village in km)	Local inquiry	Helps in selection of appropriate schemes/ activities
12. Financing by other institutions	No. of farmers / Loan outstanding / Loan Over due	% of recovery to demand / No. of defaulters / Distance from village.
(i) Co-operative Societies (ii) Land Development Bank (iii) Other Commercial Bank (iv) RRBs	Respective financial institution	General information about functioning of other financial institutions Indicates extent of coverage Useful for working out credit gap prevalent in the village indicating level of future scope for the branch
13. Has any loan already been granted by our Bank in the village? Please indicate the number of accounts, total limits sanctioned, present aggregate outstandings, overdues and percentage of recovery to demand.	Own records	

1	2	3
14.(i) Are the various inputs like certified seeds, pesticides, fertilizers etc. locally available? If not where available? (ii) Facilities available for soil testing and water analysis (if not available at the village, state the nearest place with distance) (iii) Facilities available for storage/cold storage plants/ warehousing (State/Centre/ Private). (iv) Procuring and processing agencies in the area (Public and private) such as sugar mills, tobacco companies etc. (v) Marketing societies and other marketing agencies.	(i) Local inquiry (ii) Agrl. Extn. Officer at Block level (iii) Agricultural Assistant/VAW	Indicates general level of development and infrastructural support available. Should be taken into account while planning for crop loan activity and other schemes/ activities such as fisheries, etc.
15.(a) The group water shed in which village is located as per groundwater survey (b) Number of additional feasible wells in the group water shed as recommended by groundwater survey	(i) Groundwater Survey (ii) Minor Irrigaation Deptt. at Block/ district	(i) Scope for additional (irrigation potential through wells (ii) Scope for financing wells and pump sets (iii) Prospect for improvement in crop pattern and further crop loans
16. Village land utilisation statistics: (i) Total geographical area (ii) Total cropped area (iii) (a) Double cropped area (b) Area irrigated (iv) Cultivable waste, i.e. land fit for cultivation but not taken up or not cultivated for some years	(i) Agril. Extn. officer at block level (ii) Agriculture Assistant/VAW	(i) Proportion of cropped area to total area indicates importance of cropping. If it is very low (e.g., in the Himalayan region), plan has to give importance to other sector like horticulture,

1	2	3
(v) Area not fit for cultivation		social/farm forestry etc. (ii) Scope for further extension of cultivation, if cultivable area is available and consequent crop loan activity (iii) Double cropping is one of the indices of agricultural development. Further scope to increase double cropping may be determined in relation to irrigation potential. (iv) Scope for waste land development
17. Rainfall — Season-wise: Kharif — Rabi-Summer for the last 5 years with details of drought and other unusual conditions, if any.	(i) Gram panchayat (ii) Agriculture Assistant/VAW (iii) AEO at block level	Determines crop pattern and influences choice of new crops and availability of groundwater potential
18. Crops grown Khrif (a) Cereals (i) Rice (ii) Wheat (iii) Maize (iv) Jowar (v) Bajra (b) Pulses (c) Oil seeds (d) Vegetables (e) Spices (f) Fruits (g) Others including cash crops like cotton, jute, etc. (specify)	(i) Gram Panchayat (ii) Agriculture Assistant/VAW (iii) AEO at block	(i) One of the indicators of development of village, modernisation of agriculture and choice of technology. (ii) Indicates need for extent and type of irrigation, fertilizers, pesticides, etc. (iii) Scope for changing the cropping pattern and introducing new varieties. (iv) direct bearing on crop loan

1	2	3
Total		
Rabi		
(a) Cereals		
(i) Rice		
(ii) Wheat		
(iii) Maize		
(iv) Jowar		
(v) Bajra		
(b) Pulses		
(c) Oil seeds		
(d) Vegetables		
(e) Others including cash crops like cotton, jute, etc.(specify)		
Total		
Summer		
(a) Vegetables		
(b) Other crops (specify)		
Perennials		
(a) Fruits		
(b) Sugarcane		
(c) Banana		
(d) Other crops(specify)		
Total:		
Grand Total		
Other Statistics:		
Animals: (i) Bullocks (ii) Buffaloes of breedable age (iii) Cows of breedable age (iv) Sheep (v) Goats (vi) Poultry	(i) Gram Panchayat (ii) Agriculture Assistant/VAW (iii) Veterinary/Livestock deptt. at block level (iv) AEO at block level	(i) Scope for finance for bullocks *vis-a-vis* extent of cultivable land and cropping pattern (ii) Scope for development of dairy and poultry (iii) Cattle population indicates number of possible Gobar Gas Plants

1	2	3
		(iv) Scope for Development of other allied activities like goat and sheep rearing
Appliances: (i) Tractor/Power tillers (ii) Oil engines (iii) Electric motors (iv) Cane crushers (v) Threshing Machines (vi) Sprayers/dusters (vii) Other appliances	(i) Agriculture Assistant/VAW (ii) AEO at block level	Indicates level of farm mechanisation and future scope in relation to cropping pattern, HYV crops, level of irrigation and size of land holding.
Marketing arrangements for buying and selling of animals/appliances/products	Local inquiry	Selection of schemes/activities gets limited by the availability of marketing facilities - both for buying and selling.
19. Present level of production costs and income per hectare of some principal crops in the village: Expenses on: Seed Fertilizers Pesticides Labour costs Interest on borrowed funds Other costs Total costs Income: Average yield Rate Total receipts Surplus per hectare Remarks	(i) Local inquiry (ii) Agriculture Assistant/VAW (iii) AEO at block level	(i) Indicates viability of various crops grown and hence facilitates selection of appropriate crops for extending loans (ii) Broadly reflects on scale of finance for different crops and helps in roughly working out quantum of crop loan requirements for each village.
20. Artisan/cottage/village industries/service units	(i) Gram Panchayat (ii) Official of	(i) Indicates range of activities and helps in working out their

1	2	3
(a) No. of Handlooms	DIC at block level	finance requirements
(b) No. of silk textile units (spinning & weaving)	(iii) Local inquiry	(ii) Scope for introduction of new crafts/trades depending upon availability of raw materials and demand for produce
(c) No. of Cotton Spinning/Weaving units		(iii) Need for marketing arrangements
(d) No. of Khadi units		(iv) Level of concentration of these activities is indicated.
(e) No. of village oil *ghanis*		
(f) No. of shoe-making units		
(g) No. of leather workers		
(h) No. of carpentry units		
(i) No. of blacksmithy units		
(j) No. of goldsmithy units		
(k) No. of wood workers		
(l) No. of bamboo workers		
(m) No. of metal workers		
(n) No. of coir workers		
(o) No. of *gur* making units		
(p) No. of hand-made paper units		
(q) No. of cottage match units		
(r) No. of village pottery units		
(s) No. of toy making units		
(t) No. of household processing units		
(u) No. of other handicrafts		
(v) No. of other industrial units (specify)		
(w) No. of industrial/vocational training institutions		
Others		
Electricians	Local inquiry	(i) Indicates level of concentration of these profession.
Pumpset Repairer (Diesel)		(ii) Scope for financing
Electric Motor Repairers		
Bicycle Repairers		
Tractor Repairers		
Other (Specify)		

Traders	**No. of Units**	**No. of Persons Engaged**	Local inquiry
General Merchants			
Specialised Traders(if any)			
(i) Cloth			(i) Level of concentration
(ii) Drug Stores			(ii) Scope for financing
(iii) Agriculture Inputs			

1	2	3
(iv) Others (specify)		
21. Board indication of the activities which can be supported by credit		
Nature of activity Agricul-ture & allied activi-ties Unit cost No. of Units	(i) Local inquiry (ii) Gram Panchayat Agril Assistant/ VAW (iii) AEO at block level (iv) Official at DIC at block level (v) BDO	(i) Assessment of financial re-quirement for various purposes (ii) Scope for in-troducing new activities/en-couraging addi-tional units whenever required
(i) Sinking of new wells		
(ii) Renovation of old wells		
(iii) Electric motors pumpsets/oil engines pumpsets		
(iv) Purchase of tractors		
(v) Purchase of Milch animals		
(vi) Other term loan (items not covered above		
(vii) Crop loans		
Non-farm sector Specify activity	**No. of units**	
22. Other comments and recommendations:		
(i) Nature of backward and forward linkages, other infrastructural support available for improvement.	Local inquiry, personal know-ledge and own judgement	
(ii) Potential for deposit mobilisation including foreign remittances.		
(iii)		
(iv)		
(v)		

To Facilitate the Job of Data Collection

The nature of data which is normally available from some major sources is listed below. This may act as a ready reference for the Branch Manager to understand the items of data to be collected from each source.

To illustrate, the Gram Panchayat will be able to provide information with regard to Facilities available (Sl. No. 3 in Proforma), Population details (Sr. No. 4) and so on.

Source	Sl. No. of Data in the Proforma
(a) Gram Panchayat	3, 4, 9, 9(a, b & c), 17, 18 (Crops, Animals and Appliances), 20, 21.
(b) Agriculture Assistant/ Village Agriculture Worker	4(ii), 5, 6(A), 7, 9, (a, b & c), 14, 16, 17, 18 (Crops, Animals, Appliances), 19, 21.
(c) Agricultural Extension Officer at Block Level	4(ii), 5, 6(A), 6(B), 7, 9, 9(a, b, & c), 14, 16, 17, 18, (Crops, Animals & Appliances), 19, 21.
(d) Veterinary/Animal Husbandry/ Livestock Department at Block/Village Level.	9, 9(a, b & c), 18(particular of animals)
(e) Industries Promotion/Extension Officer DIC Official at Block Level	4(ii), 9, 20, 21.
(f) Census Data	4(i), 4(ii)
(g) Minor Irrigation Department	6(A), 6(B), 9, 15
(h) Ground Water Survey	6(B), 15

The information contained in the proforma is intended to facilitate the branch manager to identify the potentialities for development in each village and the extent of credit to be extended for financing different activities in each village, such as crop loan, irrigation schemes, dairy/poultry schemes etc. The items relevant for preparing the plan relating to each activities have not been chronologically arranged in the survey proforma. Hence to facilitate the Branch Manager's job, data items relevant to major activities are compiled below:

Scheme	Sl.No. in the Proforma	Particulars
(a) Crop Loan	4(ii)(a)	Occupational pattern
	5	Land Holding
	6 (A & B)	Irrigation
	7	Soil type
	9	Special Development Programmes
	11	Market centre
	14	Infrastructural support
	15	Water shed
	16	Land utilisation statistics
	17	Rainfall
	18	Crops grown, Animals, Appliances, Market
	19	Production cost and income for various crops
	20	Availability of agricultural inputs
	21	Activities requiring credit
(b) Irrigation (Dugwell, Tubewell, Tank, Pumpset etc.)	5	Land holding
	6(A & B)	Irrigation
	9	Special development programme
	14	Infrastructural support
	15	Water shed
	16	Land utilisation statistics
	17	Rainfall
	18	Crops grown
	20	Service units
	21	Activities requiring credit
(c) Agricultural Appliances like tractors, power tillers, threshers, sprayers, dusters etc.	4 (ii) (a)	Occupational pattern
	5	Land holding
	11	Market centre
	16	Land utilisation statistics
	18	Crops grown, Appliances, Market
	20	Service units
	21	Activities requiring credit
(d) Bullocks & Bullock Carts	4 (ii) (a)	Occupational pattern
	5	Land holding
	16	Land utilisation statistics
	18	Crops grown, Animals, Market
	21	Activities requiring credit

1	2	3
(e) Dairy	4 (ii) (b & c)	Occupational pattern
	6 (A & B)	Irrigation
	9	Special Development Programme
	11	Market Centre
	14	Infrastructural support
	18	Animals, Market
	21	Activities requiring credit
(f) Poultry	4 (ii) (b & c)	Occupational pattern
	9	Special Development Programme
	11	Market centre
	14	Infrastructural support
	18	Animals, Market
	21	Activities requiring credit
(g) Other allied agricultural activities such as goat and sheep rearing, sericulture, piggery, pisciculture, beekeeping, etc.	4 (ii) (b & c)	Occupational pattern
	9	Special Development Programme
	11	Market Centre
	14	Infrastructural support
	18	Animals, Market
	21	Activities requiring credit
(h) Village and Cottage Industries and Artisans	4 (ii) (d)	Occupational pattern
	9	Special Development Programme
	11	Market centre
	14	Infrastructural support
	18	Crops grown Market
	20	Range of present activities
	21	Activities requiring credit
(i) Trading Activities	4 (ii) (d)	Occupational pattern
	9	Special Development Programme
	11	Market centre
	14	Infrastructural support
	18	Crops grown, Market
	20	Trading units/activities
	21	Activities requiring credit

Before concluding this part, it is necessary to clarify that as far as possible, efforts should be made to collect data from the sources available at the village level (including the government functionaries). However, certain types of information may not be available at the village level, and may have to be procured from the government officials working at the block/district head quarters and secretariate. The lead bank officer of the district should extend necessary help to branch managers in obtaining such data.

10

INDUSTRIAL DEVELOPMENT IN A HILLSIDE CITY OF THE HIMALAYAS: A Case Study of Nainital, Uttar Pradesh India*

R.K. Dar and V.S. Singh

Nainital and Its Environs

A few hours drive from the hot plains of northern India, Nainital (Goddess Naini's lake) evokes the image of a tranquil Himalayan temple situated at the far end of a dark green, kidney-shaped lake, in a pleasantly cool place, at an altitude of 1939 m above sea level.

Nainital lake is surrounded by sharply rising mountain ridges which reach to altitudes ranging from 2100m to 2500m and are dominated by Naina peak, at an altitude of 2611m. An open ground behind the Naini temple, known as the Flats, provides depth to the perspective. The scenic charm is accentuated by the sudden surprise of sighting the lake at eye-level on negotiating the last bend.

Originally, an ancient religious pilgrimage place of the Kumaon region, Nainital was discovered by the colonial administrators in the 1840s as a summer recreation location. Soon after India's First War of Independence in 1857, it was chosen as a seat of the government of the then North West Province of British India. Kumaonis inhabiting the larger town of Almora, at a distance of 70 km in the interior, speedily took up habitation and business in this new settlement. A Municipal Board was formally constituted in 1850. The metre-gauge rail-head of Kathgodam was constructed by 1889. By 1905, Nainital was carved out as a separate district. The first major school for girls had come up in 1878, and for boys in 1888-89. The district hospital was set up in

* The views expressed in this paper are those of the authors and do not reflect government policy or commitment.

1892. A magnificent mansion, designed like a Scottish castle, was completed for the Lieutenant Governor in 1900, with a campus area of over 200 ha. The settlement was now complete. The census of 1901 recorded a population of 7609.

The motor road from Kathgodam to Nainital was completed in 1915. Health sanitoriums were set up in Bhowali and Gethia, respectively in 1912 and 1953.

The charm of Nainital region was greatly enhanced by the remarkable occurrence of a number of other lakes in the neighbourhood of the town, within a radius of 23 km.

Relevant data on dimensions and altitudes of these lakes are shown in Table 10.1.

TABLE 10.1: **Lakes in the Nainital Region**

Location	Altitude (m)	Surface Area (km^2)
Nainital	1938	0.48
Khurpatal	1600	0.39
Sattal	1367	0.40
Bhimtal	1331	0.85
Naukuchiatal	1220	0.45

A few words regarding the characteristics of the geographical area and nature of terrain would be in order. Broad physiographic features of the Nainital region are (a) typical outer Himalayan formation, (b) relatively high altitudes around Nainital town, (c) compact catchment areas of the succession of lakes. The area, on an average, reflects a highly rugged terrain. Lithologically, it consists of calareous slaty shales, characterised by lenses of dolomitic limestone. The physico-chemical characteristics of the rocks around Nainital are such that the bed rock can be easily weathered and a large amount of sediment be available. On the contrary, the quartzites, massive volcanics and silicious limestones present in Bhimtal area are not easily amenable to weathering process.

Demographic Features

At the time of the first post-Independence population census in 1951, Nainital town still had a permanent population of only 12,350 inhabitants. This was almost ten times the population of the next largest settlement of Bhowali (1302) in the neighbourhood. The town continued to dominate the mountainous sub-region as is evident from the fact that the total population of the 35 villages and two other towns in the periphery of Nainital, lying within the area covered by the Greater Nainital Development Authority (GNDA) established in 1984, remained less than that of Nainital town itself (Table 10.2).

TABLE 10.2: Area and Population of Greater Nainital Development Authority Region, Year 1951 and 1981

	Geographical Area (in ha)	Population size 1951	Population size 1981
1. Nainital	500 (11)	12,350 (55)	24,835 (54)
2. Bhowali	130 (3)	1,302 (6)	3,212 (7)
3. Bhimtal	396 (9)	(*)	2,871 (6)
4. Rural (35 villages)	3,508 (77)	8,652 (39)	15,138 (33)
Total:	4,534 (100)	22,304 (100)	46,056 (100)

(*) included under Sl. No. 4. Rural.

At the same time, other demographic characteristics have changed significantly in the GNDA region over the last three decades :

(a) Population growth rates peaked in 1971, but tapered off by 1981. There are visible signs of resurgence in the eighties. The precise trends would be revealed only after the census data for 1991 are analysed.
(b) Average household size increased from about four to nearly 50 in Nainital town.
(c) The ratio of workers to non-workers declined sharply in the rural areas, on account of out-migration of active population to areas outside the GNDA, and likely diversion to education.
(d) Non-farm workers increased rapidly from 56 per cent to 85 per cent of the work force in the region; even in the rural areas, the share of non-farm workers increased from 25 per cent to 62 per cent, signalling a marked diversification of occupations.

The rapid acceleration in the size and density of population in Nainital town and GNDA region since 1951 is clearly visible from

Table 10.3.

However, the change in the rest of the district is even more radical, especially in the plains area where extensive marshy lands were reclaimed and the green revolution produced remarkable impact.

TABLE 10.3: Population Growth Rate and Increase in Density

	Annual growth rate of population (%)		Population per ha of gross area		
	1901-51	1951-81	1901	1951	1981
Nainital town	0.97	2.36	15	25	50
GNDA region	*	2.45	*	5	10
Nainital district					
(a) other hill areas	*	2.16	*		2.41
(b) plain blocks	*	4.71	*		4.21

* not readily available

In addition to the normal increase in non-farm workers employed in services and trading operations related to the upkeep of the local population, major increases took place in the government and local bodies sector, education, and in industry, especially the tourist industry.

Focus on the Central Core Area

In view of the central significance of Nainital town to the region, a closer examination of its situation is called for. Nainital town has a total area of 11.73 km², with the following land use pattern (Table 10.4).

TABLE 10.4: Landuse in Nainital Town

Item	Percentage share
(a) Lake	4
(b) Residences, schools, offices	32
(c) Hotels	13
(d) Open	51

The open area is mostly the lake catchment, which has unusual slope characteristics and is managed by the forest department Table 10.5.

TABLE 10.5: Features of the Open Area in Nainital Town

Slope (degree)	Area (%)	Cover (%)	Predominant cover variety
0-14	12	8	grasses and shrubs
15-35	36	32	grasses
36-70	50	60	oak and conifers
71-90	2	0	blank.

Combined with the rock characteristics, slopes, small crown cover of oaks and conifers, is the feature of over 200 cm/year rainfall which is concentrated mostly in the monsoon period from July to September. Practically half the area of the Nainital lake basin is covered with debris generated by mass movement; the entire north-western parts of the township is located on a succession of landslide debris fans. On 18 September 1880, after a prolonged heavy rainfall (84 cm in 36 hours), a great landslide took place which killed 143 persons and created the Flats. Several incidents have been recorded in the history of the town : in fact, boulders and rubble have been periodically coming down, currently since September 1987 as a result of erosion at the top of Naina peak itself. Alive to the dangers, the colonial administration had created a system of 71 drains and 235 branches, which have a continuous record of happenings for over sixty years. This terrain is currently under great stress on account of sheer human pressure, collapse of individual sense of responsibility, and a weak social regulation and enforcement system.

The Tourist Industry

On top of growth of the permanent population and its ecological fragility, Nainital town is experiencing in recent years an unprecedented summer season flood of domestic tourists. On the supply side, this reflects the natural attractiveness of the region as well as the absence of other developed tourist towns within easy reach of the hot north Indian plains. On the demand side, this rush is the product of the high growth rate of the Indian economy in the 1980s and, equally, the emerging life-style of a new, upwardly mobile, business and professional class.

Tourism department officials claim that the number of arrivals has kept up a steady increase from 3,86,000 in 1970 to 5,48,000 in 1988, i.e. an annual increase of around two per cent. However, these are figures of toll tax paying passengers, which include a stable proportion of persons visiting the district headquarters for government work, other business, delivery of supplies and services to the town population, social and personal visitors, and so on. Also included are fair-weather friends and relatives of extended families of local residents who crowd in as house guests during summer and take up every little space in private homes.

Firm figures of arrivals of tourists who use commercial accommodation in Nainital are not available but the tourism department estimates suggest that the hotel and guest house bed-strength of about 4300 records an occupancy of 55 per cent over the year.

Keeping in view other local factors, like the exodus of the permanent population when educational institutions close for winter vacations and several offices shift to the foothills, the following broad distribution of daily arrivals may be estimated for the different seasons.

TABLE 10.6: Inter Seasonal Variations in Visitors to Nainital Town 1985-88

Season	Average daily arrivals			
	Business	House guests	Tourists	Total
Spring (Feb-Apr)	300	125	749	1174
Summer (May-July)	600	300	1345	2146 (peak 3077)
Monsoon/Autumn (Aug-Oct)	300	75	600	975
Winter (Nov-Jan)	250	75	546	871

The summer peak season lasts for about five weeks, and there are milling groups of people everywhere (about 80% of the tourists belong to the upper middle class and travel in family or informal groups), cars choke up all roads, essential civic services nearly break down, noise and pollution levels shoot up. The entire system comes under the most severe strain.

While these developments were taking place in Nainital town, the GNDA region registered only marginal progress. Comparative data indicates that whereas the number of hotels and guest houses in Nainital town increased from 25 in 1947 to 68 by 1970 and 146 by 1988, the increase in the rest of the GNDA region was from a figure of one in 1947 to two in 1970 and nine in 1988. The total bed capacity in the region outside Nainital stood at 262. In most new suburban locations, an active public sector pioneering role has been noted.

Actually, for the tourists visiting the GNDA region, Nainital remains the central point from where suburban tours and day trips, picnics etc. are organised. There is no study to indicate the kind of demands that are made on the outlying tourist infrastructure in so far as use of overnight accommodation is concerned. It may be presumed that tourists who do not find satisfactory accommodation in Nainital are willing to stay in sub-region close to the town, so as to be able to return to Nainital for utilising its many attractions, specially for family groups and children, like boating, sight seeing, entertainments, variety of foods, shopping and so on.

Promotion of other Industries

Since Nainital is very crowded on account of the tourists, only a few small scale and cottage industries have taken root there, mainly for producing souvenirs for tourists, made of drift wood and pine, decorative wax candles, and for sale of speciality woollen articles which are produced in the hill region. All the rest of the goods sold are brought in from outside. However, the region outside Nainital has been actively promoted for medium and small scale industries, some of which have thrown up a successful methodology for employment creation and use of local skills.

Industrial development policy in India has constantly stressed the role of the small and informal sector of industry in promoting dispersed industrial activity and employment. A variety of supports have been extended to this sector, consisting of schemes for advance of concessional loans, hire purchase, training of entrepreneurs and workers, differential taxation, allotment of scarce raw materials, provision of land and worksheds in industrial estates on outskirts of towns, reservation of certain lines of production, and so on. In addition, identified backward districts including the hill district of Nainital, have been entitled to additional concessions, namely — (i) 25 per cent subsidy on total capital investment up to a ceiling of Rs. 2.5 m, relaxed up to Rs. 5m for electronics; (ii) a transport subsidy of 75 per cent on road transport costs of raw materials and finished goods from the nearest broad-gauge rail head to the location of the units; (iii) concessional land and workshed allotments; (iv) interest concession of one per cent on term loans; and (v) exemption in sales tax for seven years (as against five to six per cent in non-hill backward districts).

Assistance to the industrial sector is extended through a District Industries Centre (DIC), which attempts to coordinate delivery of support services on single window basis. Promotion of the electronics industry in the hill region, which has natural advantages of a dust-free, low temperature environment, and a negligible negative environmental impact, is attempted through a number of additional measures. A common facility has been created for electronic testing and development in the industrial estate at Bhimtal, and a training centre for adapting lower level technical personnel to electronics industry requirements has also been set up. Public sector companies have joined hands to set up pioneering units. One scientific organisation has set up, with government support, a training centre for small scale entrepreneurs, in what is called a nursery, making small transformers, voltage stabilizers and printed circuit boards. An industrial estate was started by clearing 3 ha of land in Bhimtal in 1962, to which an area of 38 ha was added by clearance of an old peach orchard in 1983.

Of all the areas in GNDA region, Bhimtal has the largest flat plain, which has contributed to the industrial potential of the area. This area has recently attracted one of the largest Indian private sector electronics companies, which is expected, to bring about a qualitative transformation in the regions economy.

A Special Case of the Electronics Industry

It would be an over-simplification to conclude that a flat piece of land is all that is necessary for inducing necessary change. For a period of about ten years preceding the above development, Bhimtal has seen a great deal of experimentation and sustained effort to promote industrial enterprise in the electronics field. It may be useful to note a few of the features of that beginning. A public sector company named Teletronics Ltd., a joint enterprise of a regional development corporation and a large public sector electronics corporation, started a television assembling unit in Bhimtal in 1976, for marketing through the larger company. After six years of a variety of problems, including management problems arising on account of non-availability of professional personnel in a backward pocket, the unit finally turned round through a combination of improved management and technical quality control. Currently, the value of annual production is Rs. 8m in Teletronics and Rs. 27m in a sister unit called Kumaon Television (Kumtel) which was established in 1984-85. The total direct employment provided by these two units stands at 309, including 50 women (mostly in technical category). Part of the work of these companies is given out on job work basis, presently to 60 women living in the vicinity, who were trained by these enterprises and now earn a living wage from this activity. In addition, these enterprises have given rise to a number of ancillary units run by local, lower income group families, purposely chosen and specially trained by the enterprises. These ancillary units produce television cabinets, cartons, printed circuit board sub-assemblies, cable harness, power supply sub-assemblies, audio products and sub-assemblies, transformers and coils, television and communication antennae, packing and transportation services.

Teletronics/Kumtel workers from various villages in the vicinity, travel everyday to work or take up lodgings near the industrial units.

The experience of Teletronics and Kumtel has confirmed the suitability of the Bhimtal location, and provided one type of package for hill industrial development planning; it has enabled identification of basic conditions for the success of industrial enterprises in such a setting. Bhimtal sub-region has a higher literacy rate, including among women, than most of the other areas of Nainital district. This is indicative of its early integration into a pattern of urbanisation which owes its origin to the existence of a road link since early days.

The experience of the Teletronics and Kumtel industry may now be analysed. Two types of strategies in industrialisation have apparently failed in the present setting. Firstly, the initial strategy of providing infrastructure and financial support, alongwith quota allocation of scarce materials, produced no definite direction of industrialisation because of over dependency on government supports. Under normal market conditions, such units failed to compete successfully and disappeared from the scene, sooner or later. A second strategy of creation of industrial enterprises through a base in a technical training institution also did not succeed, since commercial experience and the skills for managing industrial enterprises were not available to such institutions. The conditions required for success of industrial enterprises in such locations may be briefly outlined as follows :

(i) effective management on the spot;
(ii) training and upgrading local skills and careful selection of persons for permanent, non-permanent employment, job work, or the creation of ancillaries;
(iii) marketing and technical as well as research and design support of a large enterprise.

As regards government policy support, the public sector is dependent primarily on government equity participation. The private sector, having assessed the hill location for suitability of an enterprise, primarily looks forward to receive government support for obtaining land and nominal or substantial participation through some kind of joint or assisted sector arrangement which acts as a passport for rapid clearances through various parts of the bureaucratic system. Financial incentives mainly play the role of offsetting additional costs of a hilly location, which is liable to be distant, isolated, and, therefore, requiring a whole lot of infrastructural investments for upkeep of the industrial population (which would, in other more central locations, be transferred to some nearby urban or industrial township). It may be concluded that since the industrial enterprise is itself a major factor in promoting regional development, there is a sound economic basis for government to absorb part of the financial cost of promotion of the infrastructure required by the industrial enterprises.

Encouraged by the above experience, a public sector enterprise wholly devoted to the promotion of an electronics industry in the hill region was set up in 1985-86, called HILLTRON. This corporation is now engaged in creating industrial activities in some of the other hill districts through promoting a comparable package of measures to encourage joint or assisted sector enterprises to come up through private initiatives. In the GNDA region, an EDP ribbon manufacturing unit has come up in the assisted sector, a cordless telephone project is being promoted in Jeolikote. Mention has already been made of a major national company, which has been allotted a large piece of land in Bhimtal; another large company is now coming up for the manufacture of vacuum cleaners.

Coping with Environmental Stress

As noted earlier, the Municipal Board, Nainital came into existence in 1850. Over the years, sensitivity to the local, fragile environment was reflected in a number of regulations concerning building activity. Certain areas were completely prohibited for construction, others had stringent restrictions. With the increase in pressure of the local population and the acceleration of growth of the tourism sector, municipal authorities found it difficult to enforce regulations. While the regulations entitled municipal authorities to demolish unauthorised structures, in practice this authority was not exercised. Instead, offences were compounded on payment of quite low financial penalties. Municipal elections were not conducted for about 15 years in the recent past, leading to complaints that official administrators were neglecting to enforce regulations.

Rising public concern at haphazard and unregulated growth was reflected in periodic public complaints and representations in respect of building constructions, insufficient water supply and sewerage, opening of new motorable roads especially in some areas which were earlier regarded as unstable, inadequate garbage disposal systems, non-enforcement of sanitation regulations, and so on. The intellectuals and scientists undertook a series of studies about the Nainital lake and the neighbouring region from geological, biological, chemical and ecological angles, resulting not only in a series of high quality studies but also a state of heightened debate about the long term implications of the path on which the growth of Nainital was proceeding. Public consciousness about environmental issues facing Nainital was raised considerably through mass participation measures involving school children, educationists, and other members of society. Practical steps for taking environmental protection and improvement measures were worked out but these languished for lack of finance from domestic sources. Efforts are being made to obtain external assistance for a package of such measures.

A parallel effort was made to disperse the pressure of population and decongest Nainital town. As noted earlier, GNDA was established in 1984, covering localities along all approach roads to Nainital. However, it has failed to produce a regional development plan so far. It has ended up as a rather ineffective regulatory body without a philosophy or approach. It has no land policy worth speaking of, no series of financial instruments through which dispersal could be attempted. In fact, the GNDA was set up under an inappropriate law to begin with. These weaknesses have led to widespread clamour for the abolition of GNDA from the opinion leaders and people of the areas outside Nainital who were meant to be the potential beneficiaries of the arrangement. Instead of enabling the peripheral areas to participate in the growing business, GNDA also invited criticism by seeking to acquire prime lands for creating its own assets. This was a carry over of the philosophy of socialisation of land on the periphery of the metropolitan city of Delhi, where such acquisition by the Delhi Development Authority was originally justified so as to prevent speculative transfers and artificial rises in land prices. In Nainital region, the land owners were largely retaining their hold on the land, which was still very low priced as compared to that in Nainital town. Hence, GNDA acquisition was primarily seen as a displacement of small land owners at a time when the first glimmer of hope of development was just being spotted by them.

Industrial Policy Objectives for Greater Nainital

In order to sustain growth of greater Nainital area, a number of policy objectives can be suggested at this stage. Firstly, the lead roles of the tourism and electronics industry sector should be systematically strengthened so as to bring about a healthy mix of seasonal and full-year employment opportunities for the local working force. Secondly, detailed and accurate assessment of land capability and planning of land-use should be undertaken with a view to optimise both land values as well as enrich the natural landscape. Thirdly, a rational package of financial incentives and disincentives should be drawn up for inducing the desired pattern of growth. Fourthly, an extensive process of dialogue and mutual learning should be initiated between the planner and the community. Fifthly, the structure of the regional development authority should be altered in such a way that viable development projects can be undertaken and enforced.

In the following paragraphs, an attempt is made to provide a quick listing of the kind of steps which may be suggested for giving effect to the aforesaid objectives.

Stimulating Growth of the Tourist Industry

The core area of Nainital lake town should be enabled to function as a magnet for tourists arriving from at least three directions, and for dispersing them along axes opposite to the direction from which they arrive.

In the short run, areas along existing roads should be carefully surveyed and taken up for preparing physical plans based on proper land-use and landscaping.

Clusters as well as isolated campuses and units of housing for tourists should be planned for widest possible spread of benefits of growth of this industry among local residents.

A wide range of choice of type of habitation and accommodation should be designed and offered to tourists.

To maximise impact on local income and employment, selected local arts, crafts, products, including processed foods, should be developed on a village specialisation basis.

A variety of outdoor activities should be introduced, from ordinary trekking in the forests to adventure sports with the help of local young guides and clubs.

A medium term plan for improving access to the extensive forests areas in the region should be drawn up consistent with environmental safety and sustainability.

Promoting the Electronics Industry

The base of technical manpower should be widened through upgrading certificate and diploma level institutions and introducing electronics vocational stream at school level.

For higher level technical skills, Kumaon University should consolidate electronics and related courses at graduate and post-graduate level.

Linkages with industry and local educational institutions should be established for applied science organisations working within this area.

Bhimtal should be developed as a township for technologists and scientists, with suitable housing complexes and infrastructure.

Industry promotion organisations should initiate intensive dialogue with national level companies and research institutions for starting enterprises in the area.

Linkages should be established with villages in the region as well as in other interior hill areas for performance of job work in selected localities.

Electronics enterprises should involve themselves with community work as a symbol of their commitment to social development of the locality.

Rationalising Land-use

Village-wise plans involving private land, community land, government land, and forests should be prepared, indicating existing and potential utilisation on the basis of land capability and suitability for development.

Spatial distribution of activities within villages and between villages should be identified.

Data on trends in changes of land values should be periodically updated and used for forecasting and planning purposes.

In order to gain acceptance for village plans, and to create incentives for adherence to proposed land-use, joint or cooperative ownership of high value central commercial plots should be promoted through financial arrangements; this will safeguard against over building, and release land for appropriate landscaping, afforestation, parks and open spaces.

Local architectural designs and facades should be encouraged through subsidies and expert support.

Forest areas should also be developed as water nurseries, nature trails, environment parks, etc.

GNDA boundaries should be re-adjusted to natural micro-water sheds.

Creating Financial Incentives/Disincentives

Principles for grading of various areas within GNDA for levy of differential development charges, rates for services, fees and fines, should be evolved, with a view to encourage dispersal from the central core area.

Prohibitive compounding fees should be levied for non-conforming land-use and construction contrary to bye-laws and regulations; these rates should further increase in case of environmental degradation or development in areas under stress.

Parking fees, road use charges etc. should be raised to prohibitive levels, so that crowding and disturbance to pedestrians is minimised.

Loans provided by public sector and other financial institutions should have differential interests rates, processing costs, recovery periods etc. for encouraging dispersal of industrial activity.

Costs of industrial and commercial plots should be related to medium term growth potentials, rather than to historical costs, and should include a suitable premium for scarcity.

Fees and fines relatable to environmental degradation or pollution should contain an element of penalty.

The question of taxation of government and educational institutional buildings and premises should be examined with a view to creating a bias in favour of dispersal.

Harmonising Community and Planning Approaches

Multiple levels and forums should be created for dialogue and consultation.

The objectives and bona fides of the plans should be established on the basis of a sustained relationship.

Full access should be provided to the community to data, records, and policy formulation processes.

If possible, regulatory functions should be delinked from planning bodies, while links with development promotion agencies should be strengthened.

Consensus-making arrangements should be multiplied, specially for creating common positions regarding natural and environmental factors and constraints.

Obligations should be equally imposed on private and public sectors.

Constant improvement in the process of dialogue should be attempted.

Higher costs of the planning process on this account should be accepted, on long term economic and social grounds.

Improvement in the Structure of Regional Authorities

The structure should be related to the objectives foreseen rather than to previous municipal history or imitation of inappropriate, non-hill experience.

At the apex level, the authority should integrate development as well as administrative functions.

There should be integrated budgeting also, in order to obligate line functionaries.

The design of the authority should be evolved flexibly, and may consist of general a body, functional committees, advisory groups, executive board, chairman, depending on the specific situation in the region.

The structure should bring together not only officials and non-officials but also financial institutions, sub-national planners, non-governmental organisations, and representatives of special interests like environmentalists, women, etc.

The relations between the regional authority and national/state governments should be based on a series of mutual obligations rather than on hierarchy.

Conclusion

The Greater Nainital area is one of the several geographical regions in the Indian Himalayas which display signs of disparate development. As aspirations of local people rise and governments seek to respond through constant improvisation, hillside environments come under new stresses and strains, and face a risk of undermining the very features which created the scope and opportunity for development. The present case study attempts to capture some of the flavour of the experience in one agglomeration in Kumaon. It does not pretend to be an assessment of regional theory, nor seeks to test the applicability of any particular approach. It stresses the need to look at problems in a candid and practical manner with a view to move towards a better planning system. Enough is contained in the case study to invite discussion on the basis of the experience of other hillside cities.

The central point thrown up by the foregoing discussion is that it is not possible to create conditions for balanced regional development without a clear and full analysis of and agreement on the pattern of growth which would bring about spatial harmony and equity. This may be a difficult exercise but there is no escape from undertaking it, since the only alternative is totally unregulated growth. In fragile, hill regions unregulated growth would sooner or later lead to serious disasters. Methodologies for developing such regional plans are not available off the shelf. For a long time to come, steady progress and improvisation would be necessary to generate proper methodologies which fit one or another type of hill region.

However, certain basic features of the principles and institutional arrangements for such regional development arrangements can be identified from the experience of the Nainital region.

REFERENCES

Vaid ON, Industrialisation of Kumaon in Context of Regional Development *in Valdiya KS(Ed)* Kumaon; Land and People (Nainital : Gyanodaya, 1988)

Prasad, Ram, *Micro-industrial Potential of Outer Himalayan Hills of Uttar Pradesh*, in Singh, JS, Singh SP, Shastri C (Eds) *Science and Rural Development in Mountains* (Nainital : Gyanodaya, 1981)

Pandey GC, Developing Group Entrepreneurship for Rural Development in Hill Regions in Singh JS, Singh SP, Shastri C (Eds) *Science and Rural Development in Mountains* (Nainital : Gyanodaya, 1981).

Rawat AS & Maid OP, *Nainital : A Profile* (Nainital : Nanda Prakashan, 1983).

Khanka SS, The Population of Uttarakhand In: Joshi SC et. al (Eds) *Integrated Rural Development in Hill Areas* (Nainital : Gyanodaya, 1984).

Pant SD, *The Social Economy of Himalayas* (London George Allen and Unwin, 1935)

Valdiya KS, *Environmental Geology: Indian Context* (New Delhi: Tata Megraw, Hill, 1987).

Papola TS, *Development of Hill Areas: Issues and Approaches* (Bombay: Himalayan Publishing House, 1983).

Shah SL, *Planning and Management of Natural and Human Resources in the Mountains: A Micro Level Approach with Special Reference to Central Himalayas* (New Delhi: Yatam Publications, 1986).

Singh PR & Boojh Ram, *Environment and Hill Development* (Lucknow: Directorate of Environment, Govt., of U.P., 1988).

Singh JS, *Environmental Regeneration in Himalayas: Concept and Strategies* (Nainital: Gyanodaya, 1985).

Department of District Gazetteers, Govt. of U.P., *Uttar Pradesh, District Gazetteer, District-Nainital* (Lucknow: Govt. of Uttar Pradesh, 1979).

Registrar General India, *District Census Hand Books, Nainital 1951, 1961, 1971 and 1981* (New Delhi : Publications Division).

State Planning Institute, U.P., Economics & Statistics Division *Statistical Diary, Uttar Pradesh, 1988* (Lucknow: Government of Uttar Pradesh, 1989).

Directorate of Agriculture, U.P., *Bulletin of Agricultural Statistics, 1985-86* (Lucknow: Government of Uttar Pradesh, 1988).

Board of Revenue U.P., *Agriculture Census in Uttar Pradesh* (Lucknow : Board of Revenue, U.P., (Lucknow, 1986).

Govt. of India, Ministry of Forest & Environment, *Forest Conservation Act, 1980*. (New Delhi, 1980).

Rawat A.S., History, Growth and Decay of Nainital, A Himalayan Township (Paper presented in Save Nainital Workshop, Sponsored by Department of Tourism and Environment. U.P. Government, Nainital, 1-3 September, 1989).

Singh, SP, Issues of Environment and Development in Nainital (paper presented in Save Nainital Workshop, sponsored by Department of Tourism and Environment, U.P. Government, Nainital, 1-3 September, 1989).

Pandey Ajay, Noise Pollution at Nainital (paper presented in Save Nainital Workshop, sponsored by Department of Tourism and Environment, U.P. Government, Nainital, 1-3 September, 1989).

Joshi Mallikarjun & Pandey PD, Causes and Remedial Measures for Rockfalls and Landslides (Paper presented in Save Nainital Workshop, sponsored by Department of Tourism and Environment, U.P., Government, Nainital, 1-3 September 1989).

Sharma AK, Slope Instability, Investigating of the Krol Belt of Nainital Hills, Kumaun Lesser Himalaya (Paper presented in Save Nainital Workshop, sponsored by Department of Tourism and Environment, U.P. Government, Nainital, 1-3 September, 1989).

Pant MC, A Report on Certain Aspects of Pollution of Kumaun Lakes with Special Reference to Nainital (Paper presented in Save Nainital Workshop, sponsored by Department of Tourism and Environment, U.P. Government, Nainital, 1-3 September, 1989).

Rawat Ajay S, Environmental Scenario of Nainital (Paper presented in Save Nainital Workshop, sponsored by Department of Tourism and Environment, U.P. Government, Nainital, 1-3 September, 1989).

Dhar TN, "Off-Farm Employment in Central Himalayan Region" (Paper presented in ICIMOD Seminar, Dehradun 1986).

Pandey, ID, "Environmental Degradation and Integrated Development of Nainital Township with Special Reference to Forests" (Paper presented in Save Nainital Workshop, sponsored by Department of Tourism and Environment, U.P. Government, Nainital, 1-3 September 1989).

Dhar TN & Shastri C, "Industrial Development in Kumaon : Status and possibilities", (Mimeo) Society for Himalayan Environmental Rehabilitation and Peoples' Action (SHERPA), 1986, reprinted in Valdiya KS (Ed) *Kumaon land.*

Bajaj JL, "The Working of Industrial Estates in Nainital District" (Mimeo), Administrative Training Institute, Nainital 1980.

Joshi B.K., "Impact of Industrialisation in the Social Ecology of Hill Areas" (Mimeo), Giri Institute of Development Studies, Lucknow, 1987.

Papola TS, "Production of Woollen Carpets in Kumaun and Garhwal" (Mimeo), Giri Institute of Development Studies, Lucknow, 1980.

Greater Nainital Development Authority, Nainital, "The Greater Nainital Lakes Region, Integrated Environment Project, Part I & II" (Mimeo), Nainital, 1989.

Pant G.B., "Unemployment and Under-employment in Kumaun" (Unpublished Ph.D. Thesis, Kumaun University), Nainital, 1982.

Pant S, "Growth of Entrepreneurs in Kumaun" (Unpublished Ph.D. Thesis, Kumaun University), Nainital, 1981.

Singh, SP, "Eco-development, Guidelines and Model of Development for the Central Himalaya", (Monograph) Department of Botany, Kumaun University, Nainital, 1986.

UNESCAP, "Environment Management of Mountain Eco-system in Asia and the Pacific", (Monograph) Bangkok, 1987.

UPDESCO, "Quick Survey of Tourism in U.P. Hills", (Monograph), Lucknow, 1989.

"DRDA, Nainital, "Nainital District, Vikendrit Niyojan Annual Plan 1989-90", Nainital, 1989.

State Planning Institute U.P., Hill Division, "Statistical Diary, Hill Region" Lucknow, 1988.

State Planning Institute, U.P. Hill Division, "Interblock variations in Levels of Development", Lucknow, 1989.

State Planning Institute U.P, Economics & Statistics Division, "Statistical Bulletin, Nainital-1989", Nainital, 1989.

11

EXPERIENCE, CONTENT AND DIRECTION OF PANCHAYATI RAJ: Reappraisal and Implications*

Indian Association of Social Science Institutions

Revival of political concern with Panchayati Raj may well mark the beginning of wider effort, on the part of those who are politically and socially sensitive, to re-examine the country's basic goals and the means by which these are to be attained within the framework of democracy, keeping in view the values and ethos bequeathed by the freedom movement. At one level, the practical measures taken in recent years in relation to Panchayati Raj institutions in West Bengal, Karnataka and Andhra pradesh (and the impact achieved through them) and those envisaged in the Constitutional Amendment Bill can be seen as an interconnected sequence and as parts of a certain political process. Even if there were no additions to the Constitution, many other States would have felt impelled on their own initiative to revamp their earlier Panchayati Raj legislation in the light of new pressures.

Since the late sixties, marking the decline of political interest in the basic ideas lying behind community development and Panchayati Raj, there had not been much writing on Panchayati Raj and little serious examination of the political, economic and social factors which have operated at various levels to cause the decline. These factors can be seen to have been at work in different ways at national, state and local levels, partly independently, partly in interaction with one another. The Asoka Mehta Committee on Panchayati Raj Institutions (August 1978)

* Paper prepared for a Research Seminar held in New Delhi on August 28-29, 1989, and circulated at the International Expert Group Meeting on Decentralised Planning, held at Lal Bahadur Shastri National Academy of Administration, Mussoorie, on 11th to 13th June, 1990.

had distinguished three phases in relation to Panchayati Raj : the phase of ascendancy, 1959-64; the phase of stagnation, 1965-69; and the phase of decline, 1969-77. The third phase continued until close to the mid-eighties.

Re-opening of issues bearing, in the first instance, on the political aspects of Panchayati Raj may be expected in due course to lead to reopening of other and still more fundamental issues. These are, in particular, the priority to be given in national planning to the basic needs of the people, to human resources and social development, to the weaker socio-economic groups and to development at the regional level, specially in the more backward regions; appropriate roles of the Centre and the States and relations between them in Finance and Planning; resumption of the movement for agrarian change and the reorganisation of agriculture and the rural economy with a larger place for cooperative and social strategies and institutions; reconsideration of some of the current thinking on technological change; reaffirmation of equality as a common national goal; and perhaps also, to return, in some measure, to the philosophy of greater economic self-reliance and avoidance of excessive dependence on external resources. The current discussions on Panchayati Raj could lead eventually to other questions being asked — asked of all concerned — and thereby bestir deeper movements for national renewal.

II

Panchayati Raj might have come as a system of government at the local level but, on the morrow of Partition, the Constituent Assembly was exercised above all over national unity and the creation of a federal polity which would yet have a Centre strong enough for any contingency. The story of how Article 40 on Panchayats came to be incorporated at a late stage in the making of the Constitution, has been well documented.[1]

The idea of Panchayati Raj, as we have known it, emerged as a by-product of national planning and community development. In other words, it was thought of primarily as a means, with the support and participation of the people, of achieving rapid rural development in the conditions of a democracy in the making. It is conceivable that some years hence Panchayati Raj may enlarge itself into a full scheme of local democratic government embracing both developmental and non-developmental functions. This would seem logical, but must be a matter of evolution from within and under pressure of social forces and political movements. It is possible that in this respect some States will move first showing the way to others. At the present stage, nevertheless, the experience, content and direction of Panchayati Raj have to be considered primarily from the angle of planning and development, with emphasis on the role of the people and people's institutions in grassroots development.

Long before the appointment in 1957 of the Balwantrai Mehta Study Team on Community Projects and National Extension Service under the aegis of a Committee of the National Development Council headed by Shri Govind Ballabh Pant, ground was being prepared for the creation of what came to be known as the institutions of Panchayati Raj. Many tentative suggestions were put forward in the First and the Second Plan pending the creation of popular institutions duly established by statute. The Evaluation Report of the Programme Evaluation Organisation on the first four years' working of Community Projects and National Extension Service Blocks had also pointed in the same direction. Those administering community projects were becoming increasingly aware of the need for genuine participation by rural communities and by rural leaders chosen by the people in contrast to undue reliance on the official machinery. The Balwantrai Mehta Study Team was also assigned the task of removing certain administrative anomalies which had arisen from the simultaneous operation of two levels of rural schemes, community projects and extension projects, which stipulated different levels of outlays and, in theory, were supposed to mark two different phases of a single programme.

The Report of the Balwantrai Mehta Study Team was notable for its clarity of vision on the content of democratic decentralisation. It noted that for some years decentralisation of responsibility and power had not taken place below the State level.

"Such decentralisation had now become urgent and can be effected by a devolution of powers to a body which, when created, will have the entire charge of all development work within its jurisdiction. The term 'development' covers agriculture, animal husbandry, cooperation, minor irrigation works, village industries, primary education, local communications, sanitation, health and medical relief, local amenities and similar subjects. If this body is to function with any vigour, initiative and success, the Government will have to devolve upon it all of its own functions in these fields within the body's jurisdiction, reserving to itself the functions of guidance supervision and higher planning, and where necessary, providing extra finance."

The Study Team affirmed that 'rural development and rural welfare are possible only with local initiative and local discretion.'

On the question of jurisdiction of the proposed local body, the Study Team felt that the latter should be 'neither so large as to defeat the very purpose for which it is created, nor so small as to militate against efficiency and economy. This reasoning led the Study Team to the choice of the Development Block (roughly comprising about 100 villages with a population of about 100,000) as the effective unit for decentralisation. The Study Team visualised that by slight adjustment the Block could generally be made to coincide with one of the existing administrative units like tahsil, taluka or thana, the primary consideration being that the Block does not become unwieldy either in size or in population. To ensure coordination between Panchayat Samitis proposed for decentralisation at the block level, the Study Team recommended the creation of Zila Parishads at the district level. The Study Team noted the preference expressed by some States in favour of devolution of power to a local body with the district as its jurisdiction.

In the Standing Committee of the National Development Council which met in January 1958 to consider the recommendations of the Study Team, it was agreed that conditions in different States are varied and, therefore, different approaches to the question whether decentralisation should be primarily to the district or the Block might be necessary. The essential point was to transfer power and responsibility for development to the local people, as proposed by the Study Team. The utmost stress was placed on the Gram Panchayat, which generally covers a population of 2000-3000, and the village assembly, the Gram Sabha. Subject to these considerations, State Governments could take their own decisions, keeping the Planning Commission informed of the action taken by them.

Enactment of legislation in most of the States followed rapidly during the succeeding years. The Report on the Third Plan (1961) described the legislative and other initiatives taken in a number of States as 'the fruition of the general approach which has been regarded for the past ten years as basic to rural development under democratic conditions' and as 'a most significant step forward'. Reports prepared in a number of States on how Panchayati Raj was to be implemented were marked by a combination of high idealism and meticulous detail.

Ministers and senior officials in the States together applied themselves with enthusiasm to the task of giving the best shape possible to Panchayati Raj institutions. Thus, the U.P. Report was drawn up after careful study of developments in Andhra Pradesh, Gujarat, Maharashtra and Rajasthan. The Maharashtra Committee, which was headed by the Minister of Revenue, and later Chief Minister, Shri V.P. Naik, produced an outstanding Report (1961) which still deserves to be studied. Three paragraphs are quoted below from the Committee's Report to bring home the relevance of the thinking of the period to the effort now under way.[2]

"The people in general have yet to realise the importance of the role they have to play in building up the nation and its material prosperity, reasonably comparable to that in other progressive nations of the world. Such awareness of political responsibility in the masses is yet largely not there. The problems of basic amenities and better standards of living have not be tackled so far even in respect of elementary requirements of the people. We are, therefore, forced into a conviction that in the context of rising aspirations of the people and need for an expanding economy, all efforts to solve these basic problems by the State would not touch even their fringe unless we create appropriate institutions responsible to the people, enjoying their full confidence and capable of enlisting their real, whole-hearted and determined support.

"We think that the popular local bodies at the village, block and district levels have a vital role to play. They should be responsible to the people and responsive to their needs and aspirations, possess sufficient authority to enlarge their resources and thereby widen the scope of their work. Adequate powers should be vested in them and their functionaries to deal with their basic and day-to-day problems in a spirit of full responsibility. They should also be able to share, in a good measure, the burden of the State so that the State will be left free to devote its energy to solve bigger and intricate problems which, as we have seen in our study, could not receive the attention they deserved due to a forced pre-occupation with lesser, though not unimportant, matters of local nature. We have, therefore, conceived of an arrangement in which we might advantageously separate the State's functions into a local sector and a State sector.

"We also venture to suggest that this would be the proper time for consideration of various measures which would simplify procedures and systems followed by Government departments at different levels.

The Government organisation, which should then be more compact, dealing with broad policy matters and larger schemes, should be able to function far more efficiently than hitherto. In the process, all concerned would have to display considerable political sagacity and firmness to discourage any tendency to deal or interfere with local sector matters at the State level or through the State departments. So also, the present complicated budgeting procedure, entailing volumes of documents which bewilder a layman, cumbersome accounts and other administrative procedures could be rationalised in order to meet the reduced but vital responsibilities left with the State."

It is fair to say that, as the experience of evolving a district plan for Wardha in the mid-sixties illustrated, the financial delegations and the procedural changes needed at the State level failed to occur even in Maharashtra.[3] This was also the situation in other States. It is important that this lesson should be recalled and consciously applied under the present conditions.

III

Within a few years of the enactment of Panchayati Raj legislation, within the administrative systems of different States, resistances developed and ground began to be cut from under Panchayati Raj institutions, specially Zilla Parishads through the creation of official bodies headed by the Collector such as District Development Councils, District Planning Boards, etc. Transfer of subjects to Panchayati Raj institutions remained partial and the financial and other delegations needed remained highly constrained and incomplete. There were also new political factors at work after the general elections of 1967 and the split in the Congress Party in 1969. In substance, political circumstances operating from the Centre and also at the State level and the interactions between them led to uncertainties which, in turn, drew political interest away from and even led to a measure of reluctance in giving further support to Panchayati Raj institutions. Frequent postponement of elections, already noted in the Report on the Fifth Plan, was one of the consequences.

There is much to be learnt that would be of value in the immediate future from careful and objective research into the administrative, financial, planning and political elements of change which effectively influenced the course of Panchayati Raj in *individual States* roughly during the period 1968-69 and 1974-75. A serious and well-prepared research programme on these lines should receive the early attention of the Indian Council of Social Science Research, the U.G.C., the Planning Commission and others concerned to ensure the success of Panchayati Raj during the next few years. Through the years, we have come to learn that in relation to all basic institutional changes, behind their success or failure, as the case may be, lie complex combination of factors interacting with one another. Objective research will help identify these factors as they have worked in the past and could work again in the future, probably accompanied by some new factors. (This holds true not only for Panchayati Raj, but also for Cooperation and Agrarian Reform).

The Reports of the Planning Commission for all Plan periods following the Fifth Plan, including the period 1977-83, have reaffirmed the Commission's formal support to Panchayati Raj and stressed the role of local planning, including district and block plans. As a rule, the recommendations were not pressed into action, and such developments as took place were essentially illustrative. The fundamental reason for this was that due account was not being taken of certain developments which have been initiated from the Centre whose impact on planning in the States and at local levels can be seen now to have been more pervasive and far-reaching than was realised at the time, whether by the Centre or by the States. This aspect needs to be understood clearly at this time. Briefly, the equation between the Centre and the States has been profoundly altered as a result of the series of *national programmes* which have been launched from the Centre over a long period of years, in which Central initiatives have been supported by ever increasing flows of resources to the States. These initiatives were taken from time to time from real concerns which were felt to be imperative and seemed desirable in themselves, whose further consequences, however, were not fully foreseen or were implicitly underestimated.

IV

When planning commenced in the area of rural development, the Planning Commission drew a great deal on initiatives which had been taken in different parts of the country like the Firka scheme in Madras, Sarvodaya scheme in Bombay. Etawah Project in U.P., rural extension in Baroda, and work done at Sevagram, Sriniketan, Martandam and elsewhere. With the wartime Grow More Food Programme as its progenitor, for the first time, with the onset of the First Five Year Plan, Community Development and the National Extension Service were introduced as a nation-wide programme to be completed over a period of twelve years or so. The country was divided notionally into some 5500 development blocks and each year additional blocks were brought under the national programme. The common elements in the machinery which still largely exists at the Block level are to be traced to this important development. Community development, despite its limitations in practical working, was an enormous national undertaking and, in a sense, embodied the people's side of planning. It should be noted that though a great deal of initiative came from the Centre, specially from the Planning Commission, acting as the Central Committee (with the Prime Minister as Chairman), under whose aegis the Community Projects Administration functioned, the programme was placed squarely within the plans of States and State Governments were fully responsible for it. However, being a national programme largely "led" from the Centre, the Community Development Programme did have the effect of 'drying up' innovative experiments in rural development on the part of the States.

Early in 1961, the Planning Commission initiated two efforts — the Rural Works Programme and the Rural Industries Projects. The former emerged from close consultation with Chief Ministers on a draft scheme which had been prepared in the Planning Commission and was broadly approved by the National Development Council before it was launched. But it was yet no more than a pilot scheme. It assumed large dimensions only as part of the *Garibi Hatao* call given by the Prime Minister, Shrimati Indira Gandhi, early in 1972. These dimensions have since grown steadily into the national Rural Employment Programme and its adjunct, the Rural Landless Guarantee Programme and, very recently, into the Jawahar Rozgar Yojana.

The Fourth Plan (1969-1974) introduced a number of Special Programmes from the Centre such as the Drought Prone and Desert Areas Programme, Hill Areas Programme, and Marginal and Small Farmers and Agricultural Labourers Programme.

The Fifth Plan introduced the Minimum Needs Programme and continued on a larger scale the Special Programmes initiated earlier.

By the time the Sixth Plan (1980-85) began, the Marginal and Small Farmers and Agricultural Labourers Programme was merged into the Integrated Rural Development Programme (IRDP) and extended to the entire country, with commercial banks drawn into large-scale lending supplemented by the provision of the subsidy component from the Budget. With the introduction of the idea of reaching 'target groups' below the poverty line, the IRDP became a beneficiary-oriented scheme, its area development aspects being gradually disregarded. The approach of reaching those below the poverty line was also extended, somewhat mechanically, to TRYSEM (Training for Rural Youth for Self-Employment). A similar approach was followed in the scheme for the development of women and children in rural areas (DWCRA).

Since large funds were now being routed to Special Programmes, which fell within the operational responsibility of the Department of Rural Development at the Centre, the role of the Planning commission as well as of State Governments diminished in actual practice.

Outside the rural development field proper, similar policies were being pursued in the area of Family Planning and Integrated Child Development Services. In relation to scheduled tribes, the ITDP (Integrated Tribal Development Programme), with its Component programmes, was introduced. Likewise also for scheduled castes.

Thus, Special Programmes of various kind have now become the main substance of the country's rural development effort. Each Special Programme carried its own flows of resources, its own staff and organisational patterns and its own control and monitoring mechanisms — all concentrated in the concerned Ministry at the Centre. What used to be *Guidelines* arrived at jointly in consultation with representatives of States, gradually became *Manuals* issued by the Central Ministry. Invariably these went into excessive operational detail, gave little scope for adaptations and variations, and were narrowly controlled within the Department at the Centre through annual allotments of funds for each Special Programme.[4]

The Expert Group on Programmes for Alleviation of Poverty constituted in 1981 by the Planning Commission under the chairmanship of Professor M.S. Swaminathan was struck by several rigidities and distortions which had become part and parcel of the anti-poverty programme. However, even they did not fully realise and foresee all the implications of the Special Programmes which had taken shape over the years.[5] Nevertheless, the Group drew attention to the role of the District Rural Development Agency (DRDA) which had been established at the instance of the Centre as a registered society. The DRDAs had the Collector as Chairman, a large and diverse membership, an Executive Committee, and an approved staffing pattern. The DRDA was made responsible for implementing the anti-poverty programmes. The Chairman of the Zilla Parishad was one of the members of the DRDA. The Zilla Parishad and the system of Panchayati Raj institutions were much less than central, even marginal, to the planning and implementation of anti-poverty programmes.

The Planning Commission's Expert Group urged that conditions should be created for effective decentralised planning. This implied (a) the concept of area planning based on survey of local resources and identification of investment opportunities for raising income levels, and (b) allocation of resources according to carefully determined priorities. The scheme of integrated rural development had been initially proposed along with the 1976 Budget by the then Finance Minister, Shri C. Subramaniam, in a paper outlining 'Strategy for Integrated Rural Development'. The objective was to promote the optimum utilisation of the economic growth potential of each district. It was stressed that the programmes for individual districts should have no rigid structure. Instead, *each action plan*, should be tailored to suit local needs, resources and priorities based upon the felt needs and desires of the local community. The Planning Commission's Expert Group recommended going back to the 1976 concept of district level planning and urged that the district planning machinery should be strengthened and its capability for preparing useful area plans at block and district levels considerably enhanced. The Group's proposals for utilising voluntary agencies effectively and drawing on universities, colleges and research institutions were made in this context. In respect of the DRDA and the district organisation, the Expert Group observed:

> "The Group would like to stress that the arrangements envisaged above including the role to be played by DRDA are essentially short term measures. In the long run, the local development functions ought to be entrusted to the utmost extent possible and increasingly to the elected bodies from village panchayats up to Zila Parishads. The Gaon Sabha/Village Council should not only be entrusted with the identification of eligible beneficiaries but also with the implementation of developmental schemes. The Sixth Plan has emphasised the importance of Panchayati Raj bodies as an effective instrument of participatory development, and urged the state governments to take early steps for their revival and re-vitalisation. *The Group recommends that the Central and State Governments may put the Panchayati Raj bodies in position with*

despatch and endow them with adequate powers and resources commensurate with their responsibilities."

The important conclusions which follow from the above discussion and which are critical for the success of Panchayati Raj are:

(1) In place of DRDAs, the main coordinating and planning organisation for rural programmes in the district should be the Zilla Parishad. Where implementation has been entrusted to the Panchayat Samiti, the supervision and guidance of the Zilla Parishad would be available.

(2) Through conscious and deliberate replanning undertaken in cooperation with the States, all the Manuals dealing with Special Programmes should be thoroughly revised, freed of much of the existing detailed control mechanisms, and turned as nearly as possible into broadly agreed Guidelines. It should be for each State to turn the Guidelines into more specific Manuals or Instructions for the use of Panchayati Raj institutions. In keeping with the spirit of Panchayati Raj, considerable space should be given to each State for local planning and the needed variations and adaptations to suit local conditions, requirements and possibilities.

The Planning Commission has to take upon itself the central responsibility, in cooperation with State Planning Boards and Departments, for coordinating the effort for replanning all the existing Special Programmes, including those relating to rural development and rural employment. The canker has gone so deep that a major effort of policy reformulation, with political support from the Central Cabinet and the National Development Council, must be undertaken in the course of the next year or so, if there is to be a reasonably favourable environment for the fulfilment of the basic objectives of Panchayati Raj. This is a necessary condition for a number of other measures to be initiated within each State which are no less essential for the effective working of Panchayati Raj institutions.

VI

We may turn now to the conditions which, within its scheme of administration, each State will be called upon to ensure. Some guidance is already available from measures taken in recent years by States like Maharashtra, Gujarat, West Bengal, Karnataka, Andhra Pradesh and some others. The subject requires further consideration in individual States and in common forums where the experience and thinking in different States can be reviewed jointly in terms of broad approaches and principles.

Reference has been made earlier to the reluctance in the past on the part of State Finance Departments and Technical and Administrative Departments to provide for the necessary financial and administrative delegations to Panchayati Raj institutions. Such delegations are essential and will require unambiguous directions from State Cabinets. The question of delegations stands apart, of course, from the issue of adequate resources of their own for Panchayati Raj institutions at the district, block and mandal/village levels. (These have to be in addition to project and programme grants and loans and bank credits). It may be noted in passing that when State Finance Commissions come to consider the devolution of resources from the State level to the local level the consequent impact on State finances is bound to become a matter for the consideration of the Central Finance Commission. Cooperative multi-level planning has its necessary counterpart in cooperative multi-level financial arrangements and mechanisms.

Panchayati Raj came about, as stated earlier, as a sequel to the community development programme. The central organisational feature of the community development programme was the conception of a Block Level Team of extension officers supported by field workers for groups of villages. With the establishment of Panchayat Samities, the Block Team, including the Block Development Officer, became the executive arm of the Panchayat Samiti which deliberated and took decisions through its appropriate standing committees and then had its directions carried out by the Block team. The relationship between the chairman of the Panchayat Samiti and Block Development Officer was well understood. Over the years, changes took place both at the Block Level and at the field level such that, in the words of the GVK Rao Committee which was set up by the Planning Commission, "at the start of the eighties the block was a picture of disarray."

This condition of disarray came about through (a) break-up of the concept of the Block Team through the reassignment of extension officers to their parent Technical Departments, (b) weakening of field level workers through the Training and Visit System in agricultural administration without assignment of new field workers in their place having gone very far, and (c) induction of a variety of staff working in the Block, under different Special and other programmes, sponsored mainly from the Centre, with no links with Block administration or the Panchayat Samiti.

The subject of district and block administration has been gone into with care by the CVK Rao Committee. The analysis and recommendations of the Committee need fresh consideration both in general terms and in terms of conditions in each State. Uniform administrative arrangements are not necessary but certain essential conditions have to be ensured.

An issue which requires fresh consideration, both in general terms and in relation to each State, concerns the technical cadres which will work with Panchayati Raj institutions at the district and block levels, their relationship with the elected bodies, the extent to which they would have their own staff, or staff on deputation, and the administrative relations involved. Attention may be called here to the recommendations made by Shri V.T. Krishnamachari in his Report prepared for the Planning Commission and with support from the Ministry of Home Affairs, on *Indian Administrative Services and Problems of District Administration*. Question of administrative organisation and relationships require careful consideration in the light of developments since the early sixties and the present requirements.

Questions relating to the methodologies and content of district and block planning have been considered on many occasions ever since the recommendations first made by the Planning Commission in 1954. There is a considerable amount of documentation as well as practical experience available, both generally and in individual States. From time to time guidelines for planning in the Blocks have also been issued and the experience gained has been evaluated. Numerous Block Plans with the focus on full employment, on increased agricultural productivity, on social inputs etc. are available. Questions relating to decentralised planning have been considered from time to time. The experience and the documentation available should now be brought under fresh study in relation to recent and prospective developments.[7]

An important question requiring attention concerns training arrangements for non-official workers, including those elected or aspiring to serve on Panchayati Raj institutions.

Since, within the network of Panchayati Raj, cooperative institutions and voluntary agencies have an important contribution to make, how these institutions and the elected bodies could work together and reinforce one another to the advantage of the community, has also to be considered in the context of training and organisation.

VII

The scope of district, block and village plans was comparatively limited through the fifties and the sixties. Now local plans have to integrate the earlier ideas of the area and the community as means of coordination with a wide range of sectoral development schemes which characterise the planning experience of the seventies and the eighties. These encompass such diverse fields as technological applications for improved agricultural productivity, land water management, watershed planning and development, social and agro-forestry, services for children, action related to below-poverty groups, provision of minimum needs, community health and medical care, primary and elementary education, eradication of adult illiteracy, and many other lines of advance. All these have to be consciously pulled together into the framework of district, block and other local plans under the aegis of Panchayati Raj institutions. There have also to be consequential decisions and arrangements at higher levels to make such development feasible. Each aspect requires separate consideration from the angle of planning, technical implementation, organisation, finance and benefits and costs. The content of Panchayati Raj has now to be much richer and more varied than could be envisaged twenty years ago.

VIII

District and local planning inevitably raises larger questions about the ends and means of planning which are of great significance for the fulfilment of Panchayati Raj. There are important observations on this and related aspects in the second chapter of the Report of the G.V.K. Rao Committee which is devoted to "Rural Development and Poverty Alleviation — Some Conceptual Issues". The fundamental assumption about the nature of planning is the commitment to social justice, equality and the well-being of the entire community, with special emphasis on the well-being of those who had lagged behind or have remained weak, neglected or exploited. Within the limits of national resources and capacity, *Antyodaya* the welfare of all. The long-term plan and its concrete expression in each medium term plan have to meet these tests. The Eighth Plan becomes a still greater challenge and call for action in view of the renewed commitment to Panchayati Raj. There are several unanswered questions for the Eighth Plan itself which have yet to be adequately posed.

As suggested earlier, Panchayati Raj can only be seen as the beginning of an all-embracing national endeavour, based on foundations already laid, to

> assure to every citizen of India the right to work, to equal opportunity and to a minimum level of living

and to build up -

> 'through effort and sacrifice widely shared, a society without caste, class or privilege, which offers to every section of the community and to all parts of the country the fullest opportunity to grow and to contribute to the national well-being.[8]

NOTES

1. *Panchayati Raj as the Basis of India Polity. An Exploration into the Proceedings of the Constituent Assembly.* With a Foreword by Jaiprakash Narayan and Introduction by Dharampal (AVARD, New Delhi, 1962).
2. Government of Maharashtra, Report of the Committee on Democratic Decentralisation (1961), pages 146-147.
3. This was an effort jointly pursued on behalf of the Planning Commission by two of its Members along with Professor D.R. Gadgil, Director of the Gokhale Institute of Politics and Economics, and the Government of Maharashtra, with the Chief Minister (Shri V.P. Naik) taking personal interest at each stage.
4. Reference may be made, by way of illustration, to National Rural Employment Programme (NREP) and Rural Landless Employment Guarantee Programme (RLEGP), Manual (1986); Manual on Integrated Rural Development Programme (January 1980); Integrated Rural Development Programme and Allied Programmes of TRYSEM and DWCRA. A Manual (July 1987); and Jawahar Rozgar Yojana, Manual (Draft Guidelines), April 1989.
5. The non-official members of the Expert Group were : Shri Tarlok Singh, Shri EPW da Costa, Shri L.C. Jain, Professor C.H. Hanumantha Rao, Km. Nirmala Deshpande and Smt. Ela R. Bhatt. They were enabled to undertake field visits which threw useful light on the actual working of anti-poverty programmes.
6. Report of the G.V.K. Rao Committee (CAARD).
7. The literature on these and related questions is vast and needs to be studied afresh in the light of the requirements of Planning and Panchayati Raj during the next few years. Attention may be invited here, illustratively, to the Report of the Working Group, with Professor M.L. Dantwala as Chairman, to draw up

Guidelines for Block Level Planning (1977); followed by Guidelines for Block Level Planning issued from the Planning Commission in December 1979, and Guidelines on Block Level Plans for Integrated Rural Development Programme (Ministry of Rural Development, April 1982), Report of the Working Group on District Planning with Professor C.H. Hanumantha Rao as Chairman (Planning Commission, May 1984), and Recommendations of the G.V.K. Rao Committee (December 1985).

8. From Chapter I, *Objectives of Planned Development, in The Third Five Year Plan* (1961); in the preparation and drafting of the chapter the Prime Minister, Shri Jawaharlal Nehru, had taken a leading personal share.

12

MICRO-LEVEL PLANNING FOR DEVELOPMENT

Aneeta Benninger

Introduction

The following is a short note which discusses the role of Micro-Level Planning in the process of development. The process of planning for development should take place at two levels the *Macro and the Micro*. Since macro and micro are relative terms let me define them in terms of activities or decisions that are made at each level. At the Macro-level where one is dealing with large aggregates and making *major policy decisions* the planning goals are formulated and articulated and major policy directives are given. Aggregate resource requirement estimates are made and tools and techniques are evolved and selected for large scale resource mobilisation. Also estimates for aggregate employment generation in different sectors are given: employment is the medium through which gains are distributed to the mass of people. At the micro-level, all these aggregates have to be disaggregated in a rational manner to generate multi-sectoral production and employment which will lead to higher and higher incomes and higher and higher levels of consumption. At the micro-level then an action plan or strategy is evolved for translating the macro policy into action and the macro goals into desired impacts. At the micro level then *strategic decisions* are taken to generate impacts based on the local contextual constraints and potential. At the micro level, planning is impact oriented and flexible enough to suit the local contextual needs.

It is important to keep in mind that macro and micro level planning are two sides of the same coin and have a back and forth dynamic linkage. The decision-makers at both levels have to continuously refer to each other to prepare plans which are implementable. At the same time, it is essential to know that the skills of the macro and micro planners are different. The macro planner essentially deals with abstractions and values giving the framework within which the micro planner deals with the nuts and bolts of how to and where and how much. *In a nutshell then the micro level actions will translate the macro level goals into desired impacts or changes and planning is the process or the tool with which we systematize, direct, moderate and monitor the Macro-Micro links, i.e. translate the goals through actions into results on the ground.*

The Process of Planning at the Micro-Level

The micro-level planning process addresses itself to answer the following three questions:

1. How are goals formulated?
2. How to translate them into activities to generate desired outcomes?
3. How is the whole process monitored and apprised in order to keep it on the right track?

These questions are answered with the help of two factors viz. information and planning techniques. Information is analysed and utilised with the help of planning techniques to make action-oriented decisions at the micro-level. Quantitative data and qualitative observations form the basis of information. Information means a learned and discerning understanding of the situation. The sheer mass of information that is available creates problems and it is here that micro level planning techniques help us to query information purposefully.

Information of both qualitative and quantitative nature is needed at the three main stages in the planning process: (1) Planning stage or plan-making stage; (2) Plan implementation stage; (3) Plan appraisal and plan modification stage; this is, of course, a cyclical and evolutionary process and will be repeated at successive stages during the development planning process.

Planning or Plan-making Stage

The information required at this stage is of two types. The

normative or indicative information from the specific spatial region for which the plan is being made. This information tells us the existing levels of prevalent norms, e.g. infant mortality, maternal mortality, morbidity, life expectancy at birth, consumption expenditure patterns, etc. which indicate to us the existing level of development. (This is, of course, relative.) The second type of information needed is that of standards which are derived from the goals and indicate the level that we have to achieve in a particular time frame in order to achieve our goals.

A comparison between the two i.e. *the indicators of norms* and the *indicators of standards* will inform us what are the existing lacks, gaps and mis-matches that we have to tackle.

A further analysis of the same will also tell us what are the contextual or normative constraints and potentials and what modifications are necessary to suit the context.

Based on this, one can formulate plans which can be described as statements of expected outcomes expressed in terms of a series of integral chains that interact with each other to achieve the goals. Some inputs will depend on other to turn them into productive clusters of activities. An analysis of the inputs will tell us which are the dependent inputs and which are the supportive inputs. This will help determine which actions should be taken first, which should follow and which should start simultaneously. A simple planning technique, i.e. the use of a functional linkage matrix will tell you prioritisation as well as scheduling of activities. This will mean a more systematic and objective implementation as well as ease in appraisal.

Plan Implementation Stage

The basic information required during the plan implementation stage relates to the *integral chain* or the integral logic relating to the Goals — Objectives-Inputs – Outputs-Outcomes. Goals are expressed in terms of a hierarchy of broad aims which are further detailed out in terms of objectives i.e. what impact is to be generated, for whom, where and when. This can also be expressed as measurable outcomes, coverage in terms of people and area and the time required to do it.

Each goal is reached through a set of specified objectives and these objectives are reached through a set of product-oriented actions or inputs and outputs.

Here it is important to keep in mind that:

Outcomes	: *Measurable* changes in the condition of the specified people.
Target Groups	: *Specifiable* people for example beneficiaries, participant communities or client groups within a spatial area.
Project Areas	: Spatially *definable* geographic places to be changed within a specific time with a cluster of specific actions.
Time frame	: *Quantifiable* units of time within which the objectives are to be reached.

These components are bound together to form the measurable achievement indicators of the plan.

Here also the information needed is indicative in nature. This information is generally known as *baseline information* against which one can measure changes over a given period of time.

Plan Appraisal and Plan Modification Stage[1]

Here the word "appraisal" has been used as distinct from the word monitoring. It also should not be confused with the word appraisal which means "to place a value". To apprise means "to teach" or "to inform". Monitoring or checking is a part of apparisal.

Most of the times monitoring is viewed as a function carried out by a superior external to the context and control is exercised with the help of information about expenditure and physical output targets. We are using the word appraisal to indicate that this is an internal process of learning and changing in which all the participants of the programme are involved viz. the community the managers and the sponsors. It is a *dialogical process* where information flows both ways.

Here the kind of information needed relates to processes and operations which must be carried out to achieve the objectives. There is a sequence composed of dependent steps in achieving the programme. As seen earlier some inputs and realisations will depend on others. Analysis will firstly determine if the essential operation is being performed or not and secondly if it is according to the time schedule set out or necessary to avoid bunching up of operations at points in the management sequence, which in turn places functional overloads on individual workers or create confusion amongst beneficiaries.

It is important to note that appraisal generates information which is essential for effective and efficient functioning of the programme. This information is of two types: *summative* or impact-oriented and *formative* or input and process-oriented, i.e. what processes and strategies can be changed in the future to obtain better results.

NOTE

1. Abstracted from "Appraisal : A Development Process" by Prof. Christopher Benninger Exe. Director CDSA (1981).

13

MULTI-LEVEL PLANNING IN INDIA: Emerging Issues

Y. Venugopal Reddy*

Introduction

India is characterised by people of different races, practising a variety of religions and speaking a large number of languages. The need for transforming the economy of such diverse elements in the context of continental dimensions and colonial background led inevitably to a large measure of consensus at the time of independence on need for planning and irrelevance of giving dominance to market solutions in the process of nation-building. The economy, at the beginning of planning era, was inherited from the colonial period and was, thus, highly fragmented and distorted. An example of dualism is that about 70 per cent of all industries were located around the three leading port-towns. Thus, one of the major tasks of the planning era was to redirect capital resources and technical skills to where India's manpower and natural resources lay (Alagh, 1988). In the early phases, efforts were concentrated on laying foundations for heavy industry; instruments of developing-planning; building democratic transforming the colonial administrative structures to instruments of development-planning; building democratic institutions at local and intermediate levels; and focusing on issues of decentralised planning with special reference to the development of backward regions/ districts. However, with reference to decentralised planning exercises,

* The author is grateful to the National Institute of Planning and Economic Policy, Karl Marx University of Economics, in particular Rector Csaki in Budapest, Hungary and Professor Radhakrishna of Centre for Economic and Social Studies, Hyderabad, India, for the opportunity provided to him to present this paper. He is also thankful to his sister Pramila who typed paper overnight on a weekend in London.

in 1972, a national task force of the Planning Commission was set up (of which the author was a member) to examine various aspects of multi-level planning and spatial analysis. The basic conceptual framework for multilevel planning in India was set out by the chairman of taskforce, Professor S. Chakravarthy in his inaugural address to the task force (Chakravarthy, 1972). This paper follows up on the same conceptual framework and applies to the current situation but encompasses emerging socio-political issues also.

Defining Multilevel Planning

As mentioned in the preceding section the provocation for consideration of multilevel planning arises in connection with the need for decentralised planning. Strictly speaking, a plea for decentralisation implies that some functions which can be more efficiently performed at lower levels in hierarchy are being performed at higher levels. Logically, therefore, any plea for decentralisation implies a hypothesis about the appropriate functions to be performed at appropriate levels. The approach of multilevel planning involves capturing this hypothesis in the interest of optimal functioning of a system. In the context of planning for social change such appropriateness of both levels and functions will have to be determined in socio-political context.

There could be centralised analysis of all aspects of the system that is sought to be planned, decision-making at the centralised level and a direction from a single level. But it is recognised that there are costs of obtaining information; loss of time and difficulties of clarifying concepts uniformly applicable to all situations; problems of distortions in transmitting decisions for implementations, etc. In other words, from a purely cost-effective angle of decision-making, multiplicity of agency levels in a semi-hierarchical fashion entrusted with decision-making powers may be called for.

Further the socio-political compulsions may require that decision-making powers are distributed to more than one level for the same area. Similarly decisions can be made at different levels by the same agency or by different agencies.

It should, thus, be clear that multi-level planning is different from, though it includes, decentralised planning, regional planning, regional development and area development. Existence of multi-level implies performing different functions in terms of exercise of power within the broad spectrum of process of planning (namely, feeding information;

gent for implementation; performing delegated-restricted-decision-making functions and decision-making itself.)

In brief, therefore, multi-level planning may be defined as the utilisation of multiplicity of well defined area levels and agency levels performing well understood functions operating on the same territory and people inhabiting such territory.

Factors in Multilevel Planning

In undertaking such an exercise in multilevel planning, apart from macro economic aspects, social, political and administrative factors have to be kept in view. It is proposed to recall these factors below.

Macro Economic

In the interests of consistency and ensuring proper linkages it is generally believed that centralised approach to planning is essential. On the contrary, the importance of spatial and social context is invoked to press for decentralisation in addition to the arguments of efficiencies and costs of gathering information. For instance, in the case of mixed economy like India, a large number of production units particularly in agriculture, small industries, etc. are involved in making their own decisions about what to produce, how much to produce, and how to produce. These production units operate in a variety of climatic, social and institutional context. In such an event and to the extent planning implies essentially use of incentive and disincentive mechanisms, it is considered extremely difficult for a centralised planning agency to appreciate the variety of situations and modulate the incentive and disincentive mechanisms to suit local conditions.

Nation Building

Like the subject-matter of planning the issues of centralisation and decentralisation in planning are also essentially political in the ultimate analysis. Like all newly independent countries India is also keen to strengthen the nationalist forces and fight disunity within. This implies tendency to centralised government. With the experience gained, it is sometimes argued that the goal of nation building is better served by recognising the pluralistic nature of these societies and identifying area units by explicit recognition of distinct social characteristics (linguistic, cultural, regional), etc. and sharing the decision-makin powers.

Social

Often it is argued that decentralisation enables popular participatio and feeling of participation is desirable by itself. In contrast, it i argued that decentralised popular participation would result in mor dominant elements or feudal elements dominating. However, both i theory and practice it has not been established that the class structur of any society and its capacity to influence the governmenta decision-making would change depending upon the size of politica unit or sub-unit.

Political

It is argued that the requirement of value judgement in planning a various levels of disaggregated decision-making demands introductior of political elements at all levels. This may in turn require elections tc various levels and consequently, though not necessarily, party politics (where there may be centralisation to counter the decentralisation in the government.)

Administrative

In administrative terms, there is usual chicken and egg problem i.e. institutional structures are not developed at decentralised levels to start with. Over period, however, skills may be developed but bureaucracy has a tendency to centralise and by this process counter the decentralisation.

Dynamics

In the final analysis, the whole issue of multilevel planning should be viewed in a dynamic context to suit the changing socio-political and economic requirements. In this paper, some of the emerging issues will be tackled after narrating the relevant features of planning in India and indicating current status in terms of area levels, activities and agency levels.

Features of Planning

The three important characteristics of planning in India are that it is taken up in a democratic framework, operated through a system of federation involving concurrent planning at the national and state level and the system of planning operating within the framework of a mixed economy.

The democratic element implies that the elected governments at state level may be exposed to political and policy compulsions different from or consistent with those that hold sway at central level.

The federal nature implies certain amount of freedom for planning for each state guaranteed by the constitution within overall national framework. In a way, in planning jargon the instruments of national level are the constraints for state level and *vice versa*. It also implies emerging frictions are resolved through iterative process between centre and state.

The mixed economy feature indicates existence of millions of production units which have their own considerations in making decisions about nature, levels and processes of production. These dispersed units have to be influenced by plans of centre and states to achieve their objectives through a series of incentives, disincentives and provision of enabling infrastructural facilities — sufficiently varied to suit widely differentiated conditions in different states and different areas of each state.

While the federal nature demands planning atleast at two levels i.e. Union and states (planning being in the concurrent list as per Constitution) the mixed economy in a pluralistic socio-economic environment and size of states would require planning at sub-state levels also. Thus, multi-level planning in India has to be viewed in terms of activities at different area and agency levels extending well beyond union-state framework.

Area Levels

In determining appropriate area levels, there is need to take into account, not only planning-requirements in terms of techniques and processes but also social, political and administrative structures (Venugopal Reddy, 1979). At the time of Independence there was need to integrate a large number of technically sovereign units of varying sizes and differing structures into a coherent whole. This was done through a number of measures of redefining and consolidating tier between basic settlement (village) and nation. By 1956, (with some changes in specific units subsequently also) states have been carved out within a formal federal structure. Second, 'districts' within the state as basic unit were kept intact wherever viable with occasional changes in borders where warranted. Villages were consolidated into community development 'blocks' in early fifties on a nation-wide pattern. Formalising and rationalising the units, peacefully is a great achievement of fifties.

There are intermediate tiers also, with a view to ensuring coordination. Thus, 'zonal council' (not active) was envisaged in constitution for a group of states. In some larger states, groups of districts are under a 'division' for administrative coordination. In many states, regulatory administration is carried out by a 'taluk' (which has been redefined to be co-terminus with a development block) and they are often grouped under a 'sub-division' for administrative purposes.

Since the units below the state are entirely within the jurisdiction of state concerned, at least two states in mid-eighties (Andhra Pradesh and Karnataka) have modified the block level and introduced 'mandals' (unit analogous but far smaller than a block). This constitutes a new development.

A number of scholars (Raj K.N., Gadgil D.K., Bhat L.S., Prakasa Rao V.L.S., Chakravarthy, S., Alagh Y.K., Anand Sarup, Dantwala., Rao V.K.R.V., Wahiduddin Khan., Wanmali. S., Sundaram K.V., Misra R.P., Venugopal Reddy Y. and so on) have analysed this issue. Consensus appears to be in favour of district as a unit with varying degrees of limited emphasis on block and village. Further supra-district units are occasionally suggested for tackling special regional problems. One school (Bhat, L.S., 1970) prefers redefining borders of districts to make them economic regions while another sees no particular advantage in it (Venugopal Reddy, Y., 1979).

A large number of official committees had also gone into the issue (Balwant Rai Mehta Study Team, Administrative Reforms Commission, Ashok Mehta Committee, Planning Commission's working group on district planning, Prime Minister's economic advisory council; CAARD report; and more recently Sarkaria Commission). They also tend to support the consensus in academic circles but with one difference viz. Prime Minister's economic advisory council pleads for a level 'division' covering a group of districts in larger states but with substantial planning resources and functions. The most recent pronouncements, particularly from Prime Minister focus only on district planning as one of the major thrusts of proposed Eighth Five Year Plan.

On Activities

A ticklish problem, however, relates to the issue of activities that should appropriately be undertaken at each area level. The division of powers and responsibilities between union and states is enshrined in the Constitution. Over the period, however, as in the case of most federations, there have been tensions between the Union and States both on political and on financial — economic planes. Literature abounds in analysis of these though a formal model or analytical policy framework for redefining the activities cannot be found. However, the report of Sarkaria Commission (1988) and the working of Finance Commission currently underway are throwing up some important issues for detailed consideration.

However, in the matter of activities to be divided between State and Districts (and below), there have been substantial contributions, both in theory and practice. The first issue is whether such division between state and sub-state level should be nationally determined or left to individual states to decide. Second, whether there is need to introduce constitutional provisions to ensure continuity and authenticity to such arrangements.

There is increasing opinion in favour of constitutional safeguards for such division (for e.g. Papers and Proceedings of National Seminar on Decentralised Planning, Bangalore, 1984).

A variety of approaches have been advanced in regard to differentiation of activities viz. based on degree of linkages in developmental programmes of K.N. Raj; demand and supply approach of Chakravarthy; potentialities of development approach of Vijay Kelkar and Anand Sarup; linkages cum potentialities approach of Alagh; delegated planning by differentiating macro and micro aspects of Mathur, O.P., relative efficiency in execution of projects of Prakasa Rao, and processes approach of Venugopal Reddy.

The official committees (including Professor Hanumantha Rao's Committee of 1985, of the Planning Commission), however, focused on the techniques and procedures for formulating, implementing and monitoring district plans replicating (and adopting) comprehensive planning process coupled with detailed projectisation of plans.

Realising the intricacies involved, the Government of India has a few months ago decided to attempt model district plans under the expert guidance of National Institute of Rural Development.

On the division of activities between District and Block or Mandal there is a virtual dearth of academic or policy analysis.

On Agencies

The area levels have significance for purposes of policy only with reference to the functional agencies, their powers and inter-relations — both vertical and horizontal (i.e. across the area levels and at the same area level). For convenience these agencies could be categorised into political decision-making bodies; the planning organisation; the staff agencies (ministries); the line agencies (the government executive departments); the public enterprises; and the cooperative structure. In addition, there are number of special agencies, especially at district level, established under the societies act and in the form of government committees for integrated planning. A number of private bodies such as associations of farmers, traders, and industrialists may also be involved in the process.

Thus, in a given geographical area there are various levels of government such as centre, state and districts and several agencies of each level functioning on the same area. The relationship in each category could vary in degree from superior-subordinate, equal, semi-independent in nature. Table 13.1 gives a simplistic presentation of area/agency levels.

Without going into the complexities, suffice it to say — the way the agencies are structured at each area level in terms of representation to area — levels, and the superior-subordinate, semi-equal, or equal nature of relationship in access to resources and powers of decision-making constitute the core of multilevel planning. When the framework at sub-state level is varying and nuclear, the functioning in reality can be very much at variance with formal structure (leading to accusation of hypocrisy or real centralisation in the guise of decentralisation, etc.). For instance, elections may not be held regularly, there may be threat of supercession on flimsy grounds, there is unionisation to an extent that State or Sub-State body has no control over staff etc. However, only the more important issues that are currently emerging in this area are proposed to be described below, in terms of various dimensions i.e. social, political, fiscal and planning.

TABLE 13.1: Area/Agency Levels in India

Area/ Agency	Political	Planning	Staff	Line	Public Sector	Cooperative	Special Agencies Process	Private	Decision-making
Union	Cabinet	Planning Commission	Minis-tries	Execut-ing depart-ments	Central public sector	National Coop. advisory bodies		P	(Predomi-nant moves)
Inter-state	Advisory	Bodies[1]						R I	
State	Cabinet	Planning board or Deptt.	Minis-tries	Executing deptts. of state & branches of centres[1]	State public sector branches of centre[1]	Federating bodies or apex body		V A T	

(Contd.)

TABLE 13.1 Contd.

1	2	3	4	5	6	7	8	9	10
Supra-district	Advisory	Bodies							
								E	
District	Zilla Parishad Development Committee	District planning officers[1]		*Collector* Functionaries of state deptts. & of local body	Branches of state & centres	Federating or primary[1]	Distt. level special agency	B O D	
Urban area	Urban local Govt.							I	
Block	Samithi			*Block Development Officer* Functionaries of state & of local body	Branches of state[1]	Primary		E S	
Village	Panchayat								

[1] May exist, if there is need.

Social Issue

The major issue in the social context is the way in which the integration of the nation and its people could be brought about while respecting the social diversity, and maintaining cultural identity of cognizable sections. Thus, regional sentiments assert partly to maintain and strengthen separate identities (Assam and Punjab) or as a reaction to perceived over-centralisation in the union (Andhra Pradesh, Tamil Nadu, Haryana, etc.). The fact that most of the states where the parties opposed to national party are non-Hindi speaking, gives rise to complex — reactions. There are also underlying social forces like large additions to work force and employment opportunities being limited to few areas; geographically concentrated development of irrigation and commercial agriculture; protection, security and subsidisation of organised (particularly) public sector benefiting select groups/areas, etc. These have led to different sets of reactions in different states (for instance, rice subsidy scheme in one state, employment guarantee in another, widows pension in yet another) particularly among non-congress states. The Union feels obliged to design and ensure implementation of uniformly determined programmes to alleviate poverty (such as rural employment, housing, etc.). In some states sub-state sentiments are also tending to assert themselves. Whether strengthening of sub-state political entities coupled with greater autonomy to these sub-state levels would be a way of reconciling the nation building efforts or it would fragment further — is an important issue.

Political Issue

At a political plane, the dominance of personality — based politics tends to centralism in party and consequently though not always in governments. Democratisation of party — functioning and politicisation of government functioning are sometimes attempted to effectuate process of redefining the power equations but, in the process, the technical or rational input of planning at various levels may tend to get undermined. This complex situation, given multi-party governance of different states, has led to appointment of Sarkaria Commission. The Commission dealt at length on issues of centre-state relations covering political, economic, and planning aspects. A final view is yet to be taken on these. It has also touched upon district planning — a matter which seems to have escaped serious debate. It recommends making consultation by state planning board with district planning boards obligatory; strengthening of district and urban governments; legislation to ensure regular and free election to these bodies, and establishment of Finance Commission in each state to arbitrate over resources — allocation to districts. The recommendations fall short of three-tier federation advocated by some scholars (Mukherjee N.K., and Venugoapl Reddy Y.).

It is necessary to recognise the decentralisation of the type recommended by Sarkaria Commission may have to be part of total package of identifying and redefining relations — including the advantages and disadvantages of party – based and or direct elections to the sub-state institutions.

Fiscal Dimension

As in the case of many developing countries, India is facing serious fiscal problems in the eighties — in the Union and all States. The fiscal crisis is evidenced not only by increasing reliance on indirect taxes but also deficits on revenue account (which are now in the region of three per cent of GDP and 90 per cent of deficit on union account only), and consequent deceleration in government savings to finance planned investments. However, the overall impact of fiscal deficits affects different area — levels differently. Thus, union has options like free access to borrowings (external and internal) and deficit financing. The public financial sector in the domain of union provides a buffer for getting extra governmental resources. The states have to face the brunt of increasing social obligations (education, health, social security where roll-back is difficult) and limited options to raise resources. The latest Finance Commission, is addressing itself specially to the problem of revenue deficits in addition to vertical equity (between Union and States). There are unprecedented controversies on the terms of reference as well as methodologies proposed for horizontal equity (among States). The sub-state layers of planning and development (which will no doubt be affected) are left unrepresented in the consideration on the continuing assumption that finances of sub-state units are responsibility of states concerned.

Planning

In contrast, on planning front, Planning Commission and Union government have been closely involved in evolving guidelines for district or block level financing and creating district level agencies. etc. In the recent past, Prime Minister is meeting and addressing groups of heads of district administration (Collectors) to emphasise the importance of district level planning.

The existence and pattern of elected bodies at district and levels below is varied as between different states but in most cases, there are centralising mechanisms from state level behind a facade of decentralised democratic structures below the state level.

Further the large public enterprise sector (for instance, in a typical state, the current incomes of PE's per year is more than current incomes of government) is outside the formal inter-governmental relations. The operations of PEs (both at union and state level) are being reviewed with a view to assert enterprise-culture. This would imply that PEs will function as instruments of public policy in a more formalistic way (through memorandum of understanding and Action Plans).

In addition, liberalisation of regulations over domestic industry (licensing, broadbanding etc.) imply market orientation consistent with development strategies. Naturally the planning methodologies and processes will have to change.

The impact on social groups and geographical areas of such changed planning procedures (due to marketisation) will be highly differentiated at state and sub-state levels. Decentralisation through markets will create distortions in power balances if done without accompanying changes in powers and responsibilities among the multiple layers of governmental agencies. The Eighth Plan exercises will have to take an integrated view of state action (with reference to public enterprises, markets and levels of governments at union, state and sub-state levels).

Conclusion

The achievements of the country in transforming a fragmented and distorted economy into a reasonably coherent one with development-orientation through planned approach must be recognised. The crucial role played by the dynamics of multilevel planning framework in this process should not be lost sight of.

There are, currently as part of evolution, pressures on the system from many fronts — social, political, financial, and economic. At present efforts are focused at three planes namely —

— National level (e.g., Sarkaria Commission and Finance Commission)
— Union level (emphasis on District Planning)
— State level (creation of Mandals, state level finance bodies, etc.)

But there is need to take a total view of multilevel frame to bring these efforts within the parametres of rational institutional framework. Perhaps it is time to constitute a national commission or task force on multilevel planning with terms of reference extending to the whole gamut of social change and development.

REFERENCES

Alagh, Y.K.: 'Modelling for Indian Plans': Inaugural address to I.P.E./L.B.S. Seminar, (Mimeo), Institute of Public Enterprises, Hyderabad. Jan. 1988.

Bhat, L.S.: 'Regional Planning in India', *Sankhya*, Series B.32. Part (3&4), 1970.

Chakravarthy, S.: Inaugural Address to Task Force on Multilevel Planning and Spatial Analysis, (Mimeo), (New Delhi: Planning Commission) 1972.

Venugopal Reddy, Y.: *Multilvel Planning in India* (New Delhi: Vikas Publishers), 1979.

Venugopal Reddy, Y.: "Multilevel Planing: Concept and Pratice", in Venugopal Reddy and Kosalram. K., (eds) *Multilevel Planning, Processes and Perceptions* (Hyderabad: Booklinks Publishers), 1988.

INDEX
